50/-
O.A.
24.4.69

Anna Lysegård

 Introduction to COBOL

1968

STUDENTLITTERATUR
LUND   SWEDEN

OXFORD UNIVERSITY PRESS
LONDON   NEW YORK

Berlingska Boktryckeriet
Lund Sweden 1968

Preface

COBOL is a new and increasingly popular programming language which is specifically designed for the formulation and solution of business or administrative problems on the computer. This textbook is intended to give a fundamental description of this new language as defined in the report, COBOL, Edition 1965. The book is designed for use at programming courses on college and university level, but it should also be useful for self-instruction as answers are provided for all the exercises. I also hope that this book will prove helpful as a handbook for experienced programmers.

The essential idea behind the organization of the book has been the intention to make it useful to a wide range of computer experience, from the novice to the experienced programmer. Chapters 1—3 contain a general introduction to the computer field and may be skipped by those who have already a good command of this area. Chapters 4—8 are designed to give an introductory knowledge of the language for the beginning COBOL programmer, while the rest of the book is devoted to additional, more advanced, constructions within the COBOL language.

A fully comprehensive description of COBOL is not given in the book. Such a description would become very extensive without necessarily increasing the practical value of the book. In my opinion, the material is nevertheless sufficiently complete to cover present implementations of COBOL on computers. For complete details the manuals of the computer manufacturers must be consulted. A deeper insight into the language is offered also by the COBOL report. From this report we quote the following:

Any organization interested in reproducing the COBOL report and specifications in whole or in part, using ideas taken from this report as the basis for an instruction manual or for any other purpose is free to do so. However, all such organizations are requested to reproduce this section as part of the introduction to the document. Those using a short passage, as in a book review, are requested to mention "COBOL" in acknowledgement of the source, but need not quote this entire section.

This English edition is practically identical with the second Swedish edition. The experience gained from the use of the first Swedish edition and many helpful comments from users have been incorporated. I wish to thank Professor Roy Harris of the University of Texas for his valuable editorial assistance.

Finally, I have to confess that my work on this book has been restricted to the writing of this preface and lending my name to some of the program examples. I want to express my deep gratitude to my collaborators listed below, all working at the Department for Computer Sciences, Lund, Sweden.

Torgil Ekman
Carl-Erik Fröberg
Sten Henriksson
Kenneth Nilsson
Leif Robertsson
Axel Ruhe

Lund, May 1968

Contents

Chapter 1. Electronic data processing

1.1. Computers—an introduction

 uring the few decades that computers have existed, they have become indispensable for a great variety of human activities. The computer is no longer just an advanced research instrument, restricted to scientists and engineers. It is also a machine for everyday use, with thousands of computers standing round the world printing invoices, calculating car insurance rates, taxes, social security fees, sales statistics, production plans, and marketing prognostics. The list of current applications is very long indeed. Not only would space trips and other spectacular events be unthinkable without computers, they have in fact become a part of our everyday business and economical activities.

The first steps towards mechanical tools to do computation were taken in the 17th century by Pascal and Leibniz who constructed addition machines. The great pioneer, however, is the British philosopher and mathematician Babbage. During the first half of the 19th century he developed a number of constructions and theories aiming at devices which have much in common with the computers of to-day. The mechanical skill of his time was not sufficiently advanced to allow his devices to be completely constructed, but parts of his "engine" were completed and can be viewed this very day.

Hollerith's construction of the first widely used punched card machines provided a big step forward and they actually opened the area of mechanical data processing. The first major task of these machines was the United States census in 1890.

During World War II several different types of relay-based computers were developed in the US and Germany. They were mostly used for production of mathematical tables for military purposes. The development of electronics made the modern computer possible. The first modern computers were constructed of vacuum tubes which required much physical space and a high cooling capacity. Later on the vacuum tube was replaced by conventional transistors. During the last few years a technique with integrated circuits has become predominant; components and wires are then manufactured directly on an insulating plate. In this way it has been possible to achieve an extensive miniaturization which has many advantages such as less power consumption, greater speed, and greater reliability.

At first, computers were mostly utilized for advanced engineering and research problems. In the beginning of the 1950's they became commercially available, but it was not until transistorized computers entered the market that they were generally accepted within business and government. The production of computers has become less expensive and their speed has increased. As a consequence the price per operation has been decreasing steadily ever since they were commercially introduced. The general economy of computers is now well recognized for a great variety of applications and their use is continuously spreading into new fields.

In this book we will present a tool designed to facilitate the use of computers in business and economics. COBOL (Common Business Oriented Language) is a language for the programming of computers which is well suited for administrative data processing. This language was specifically designed to make it possible for the user of a computer to state the solution of data processing problems in an English-like narrative form. However, the COBOL programmer must be somewhat familiar with the way in which computers work. For this reason we will give a brief account of the manner in which computers input information, process it, and return the desired output information. As indicated in the preface, those who are already familiar with computer hardware may skip this description and proceed to the beginning of Chapter 4.

1.2. The problems of administrative data processing

Automatic data processing is usually divided into two main fields, scientific and administrative or business data processing. The first field is supposedly concerned with problems in which mathematical content in a traditional sense dominates. Typical tasks are the evaluation of data and the solution of well-defined mathematical problems, which usually arise from technical or scientific research. It is a characteristic of these problems that the amount of data is not very large, but the number of operations on the data is so large that a high speed computer is necessary.

The second field, administrative or business data processing, handles problems characterized by large amounts of data, which can be both numeric and alphabetic, and rather few operations to be applied to the data. Many problems of this type can be classified under the heading of file maintenance. These type applications often come from business and economic activities.

The scientific vs business basis of division is widely used and is convenient from the point of view of classification. It also has a certain correspondence in reality. However, this correspondence is definitely not complete and the division can cause serious misunderstandings.

Our first objection to the classification is the fact that many problems do not fall clearly into the proposed pattern. The treatment of certain high energy physics problems is characterized by huge numbers of data while the computer may be used for rather limited computations. On the other hand, linear optimization and other well established techniques of operations research for use in business management, often need small amounts of data while the computation is far from trivial.

Another difficulty with this rough classification is that it does not include new computer applications which are in rapid development. Fields like process control, artificial intelligence, and pattern recognition can certainly not be assigned to either of the two main domains.

The most serious objection, however, is of another kind. It is based on the increasing demand for *integration* of all information processing activities inside, say, a company. If it is possible to show a strong connection between the particular problems of information processing, then there is no reason to separate them on artificial grounds of classification. Different problems have to be treated in different ways, but the choice of method must be made bearing the global picture in mind so that no new problems arise as regards the compatibility between the different parts of the system. Later in this section we will return to the notion of integration.

In order to get a general conception about the flow of information inside a business enterprise, let us discuss an example. In fig. 1 the most important information paths in a manufacturing company are shown. The purchasing department orders raw material from a number of suppliers. The goods are received at the company, processed in the manufacturing department, stored in the warehouse, and finally shipped to the customers. The purchasing department, the production department, and the sales department supply information to well-defined parts of the process. They also exchange information between each other, and with the top management. The accounting department is supposed to handle accounting transactions and consequently receives information about purchases, production, and sales. Further it is responsible for financial transactions with the employees and the government.

We have only described some of the more important parts of the information flow inside the company. A detailed account is evidently strongly dependent on the exact structure of the company. A complete description is a time- and energy-consuming task, and a survey of this kind is indeed

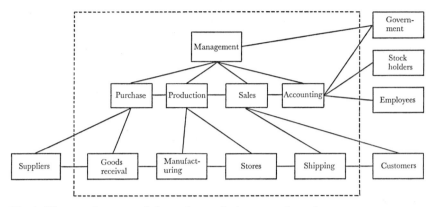

Fig. 1. The most important information paths in a manufacturing company.

the main purpose of what is called systems analysis. As a matter of fact this mapping of the communication channels inside a company which is definitely a prerequisite for any rational appraisal of the administrative structure, very often has never been done until the management starts to consider the purchase of computer hardware.

In this connection it may be wise to remember one of the most important experiences from the use of systems analysis, viz. the importance of investigating an information system in its entirety. Here again we meet the demand for integration. For example, one may be tempted to look upon invoicing or production planning as separate problems and proceed to automate them. It is easy to understand that this does not necessarily mean a simplification of the total information processing problem in the company. Any particular problem will sooner or later show substantial connections with other problems, and the result may well be that new bottlenecks or information thresholds arise between the computerized sectors and those which are still treated manually. This observation is, of course, also valid at the higher level where the company cannot be regarded as isolated from the environment but in relation to suppliers, customers, stock holders, insurance companies, government, and so on. It may not yet be reasonable to demand integration at this high level, but it is important that in planning of large information systems one prepares for future development. The work now being done by standardizing data formats and programming languages can be regarded as steps in the direction of wider integration.

We have here used the term information without a precise definition. Although such definitions exist, it will suffice to say that information is the meaning which can be assigned to data, using known conventions of data representations. By the term *data*[1] we mean a formalized representation of

[1] Following Strunk-White, The Elements of Style, p. 36, we insist that *data* is plural, like phenomena and strata.

facts and ideas which can be communicated or treated in a process. Data can be represented by symbols as letters and digits, and these in turn can be represented by different codes, for example by printed characters on paper, hole combinations on cards, or directions of magnetization in metals. Media on which symbols are stored, for example punched cards or magnetic tape, are sometimes called *data carriers*.

1.3. Elementary data processing operations

Not every problem may be successfully treated by a computer. For a problem to be placed on a computer and solved, it must be possible to break down the problem into a well-defined sequence of arithmetical and logical operations. Computers are designed to execute such operations, and to make logical comparisons to determine which of many possible sequences of operations are to be executed. In addition, computers have large data banks or memories where data and program information may be temporarily stored until required. The preparation of a computer program consists of a detailed analysis of the proposed task resulting in the specification of a sequence of operations the computer is to follow and a translation of these operations into a language which is understandable to the machine.

As an example, consider the following problem. A company with a large number of employees maintains information about its employees on magnetic tape. For each employee there is a *record* consisting of a set of data items such as identification number, name, position, pay rate, tax deductions, social security fees, form of payment, and so on. The records are supposed to be sorted on the employee identification number. All records together form a *file* which in this case we may call e.g. a master employee file.

For a given pay period there is generated a certain amount of new information about the employees concerning absence, production, etc. This information is usually represented in forms which are not immediately accessible to the computer. The data must be punched on cards or paper tape together with the identification number for every employee involved, and in this way a current activity record for the employee is formed. The computer reads these current activity records in whatever order they are collected and they are fed into the machine and temporarily stored on magnetic tape. The records will then be sorted by the computer according to the identification numbers. Sorting is one of the most frequent tasks which computers perform. In principle, sorting is carried out by comparing the *keys*, i.e. the information decisive for the sequence, for two records at a time. Depending on the outcome of this comparison, a rearrangement of the records may take place and a new sequence established. The final result of the sorting operation is a file of the current activity records in the same order as the original master employee file.

The salary computation may now take place. For each employee one record from the master file and one from the current activity file are placed in the central memory of the computer. Then a number of arithmetical operations are carried out. Piece-rates are multiplied by number of produced units etc., the gross pay is calculated and becomes the basis for tax deductions and fees of all kinds. This computed information must be preserved for various other purposes so it is stored on another magnetic tape; later on it will serve as input for other programs. The current payroll must be written out directly, so these data are edited and printed out on special payroll forms. Finally, the original master file on magnetic tape has to be updated, i.e. supplied with the most recent information about the employee. The program then repeats the computations for the next employee, who may have another type of payment using other parts of the program, but in principle the procedure will be the same.

It should be evident from this description that large parts of the program consist of data transfers. Copying of data from one part of the memory to another or between different memories is a frequently performed task, and a suitable programming language should contain easy means of description and execution of this process. Further, operations using mechanical devices like card readers, tape units, and line printers, as a rule are much more time-consuming than those involved in internal computation. If no special arrangements are made one will encounter a situation where thousands of extremely fast electronic circuits are waiting for a slow electromechanical unit. When programs are written, operations using such units, if possible, should be laid in parallel, and it is highly desirable that the programming language facilitates such constructions. We will see later that COBOL by its structure is well adapted to computer applications where large numbers of data transfers are required.

Chapter 2. Computers and their equipment

> *One machine can do the work of fifty ordinary men. No machine can do the work of one extraordinary man.*
>
> ELBERT HUBBARD

2.1. The structure of a computer

An example of the fundamental logical structure of a computer is shown in fig. 2. The *central processor* consists of the *control unit*, the *arithmetic unit*, and the *central memory*.[1] The instructions which govern the work of the computer are stored in the memory. They are retrieved one by one to the control unit which directs the arithmetic unit to execute operations on data which are also fetched from the central memory or have already been brought to special registers. A control panel (console) is available to the operator for manual interferences. As a rule, a console typewriter or a console display used for communication between operator and computer, is attached to the central processor. Almost all central memories in modern computers are of the ferrite core type; the access time (= time to get or store information) is of the order 0.2 to 10 microseconds. Many of the arithmetic and control operations work with the same speed which means that between 100,000 and 5 million operations can be performed in one second.

In order to avoid operations involving the slow external units to delay the central processor, the control of these units is often delegated to relatively independent control units. Their work is initiated from the central processor, but after such an initiation they can follow independently a number of instructions with the purpose of reading or printing data, or transferring data between different units.

Typical speeds for some common units will be given here. A card reader can read 500—1000 cards/min, while a paper tape reader reads 500—1500 characters/sec. The speeds of the punching units are roughly 1/3 of the corresponding reading units. A line printer works with lines containing 100—160 characters and can print 600—1200 lines/min. A console typewriter will print 10—15 characters/sec. From these figures it is evident that

---

[1] Other names used instead of central memory are *internal storage* and *core store*.

13

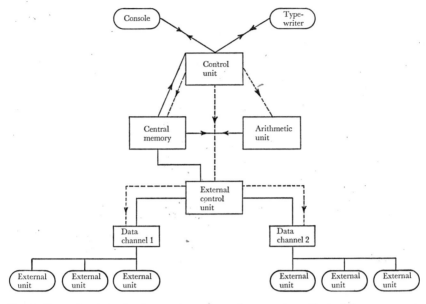

Fig. 2. Example of the fundamental structure of a computer. Dashed lines represent control, continuous lines represent information transmission.

there is a wide variety in the speed of data transmission in the various parts of the computer. The user of a particular computer should be aware of the capabilities of each part of his machine.

2.2. Data representation

In electronic computers information is almost without exception stored in *binary* form in one way or other. Nature has few physical phenomena which offer more than two stable equilibria, while there is a multitude of such giving just two. Metals can be magnetized in one direction or the other, relays can be open or closed, transistors cut-off or not. As symbols for such extremal values the *binary digits* 0 and 1 are used. These characters have in this connection nothing to do with the traditional decimal digits 0 and 1.

It is customary to represent letters, digits, and other characters by a group of 6—8 bits (bit = binary digit). A group of eight bits is sometimes called a byte. With e.g. six bits, $2^6 = 64$ different symbols can be represented. However, still one digit is often added as a so-called check or parity bit. This is put equal to 0 or 1 so that, for instance, the total number of ones in the group always becomes odd. Thus, such bits can be used for an automatic check that groups have not become subject to errors during transmission.

Another method of representing characters is by a two-digit alpha-numerical code, a method which is often used in so-called decimal computers. Here the memory structure is such that the digits 0 to 9 can be represented directly while letters and other characters are represented by two-digit combinations.

Further, there is the pure binary notation where all numbers are given directly in the binary number system. If we use a pure binary system, a special code system is necessary for information other than numbers. Other characters can be separated from binary numbers only by the way they are used.

The internal character representation on computers of different design is associated with the structure of the memory. It is common to make a distinction between fixed and variable word-length computers. In the former case the memory is organized in such a way that the smallest addressable, i.e. directly accessible, unit is a *word* consisting of a group of a fixed number of digits, for example 10 decimal digits (IBM 7070), 60 binary digits (Control Data 6400). In order to reach individual digits or groups of digits, special measures have to be taken, usually by shift operations where the digits first are separated and then moved a suitable number of positions inside a word. If the word length is insufficient for some types of information, the program has to be constructed so that several words are treated together. In variable word-length computers, which can also be characterized as machines with an extremely small word length (6—8 bits), every character is directly adressable. Information in adjacent character positions is regarded as a unit provided there is no special word mark in one of the binary positions of the character (IBM 1401) or a special character denoting the end of a group (RCA 501). It may be mentioned that several modern computers ("third generation") for example IBM System 360 and Control Data 3500 have structures allowing them to be used both as fixed and variable word-length machines. In any case, in all kinds of programming, even when advanced programming languages are used, one has to consider the internal memory structure. We will return to this problem later.

2.3. Punched cards and punched paper tape

Punched cards and punched paper tape are the dominant means for transmission of information to computers. Intense development work is going on to produce new means, among other things to make human speech and writing understandable to computers. However, we will here restrict ourselves to the two traditional data media mentioned above.

Punched cards are made out of cardboard and exist in several versions. The most common type is illustrated in fig. 3. The card has 80 columns and

ADD 600 TO TIME-AFTER-ADAM.

PAGE	SE-RIAL	CONT	A.	B.	COBOL STATEMENT	IDENTIFICATION

```
0 0 0 0 0 0 0 0 0 0 0 0 0 0 0 0 0 0 0 0 0 0 0 0 0 0 0 0 0 0 0 0 0 0 0 0 0 0 0 0 0 0 0 0 0 0 0 0 0 0 0 0 0 0 0 0 0 0 0 0 0 0 0 0 0 0 0 0 0 0 0 0 0 0 0 0 0 0 0 0
1 2 3 4 5 6 7 8 9 10 11 12 13 14 15 16 17 18 19 20 21 22 23 24 25 26 27 28 29 30 31 32 33 34 35 36 37 38 39 40 41 42 43 44 45 46 47 48 49 50 51 52 53 54 55 56 57 58 59 60 61 62 63 64 65 66 67 68 69 70 71 72 73 74 75 76 77 78 79 80
1 1 1 1 1 1 1 1 1 1 1 1 1 1 1 1 1 1 1 1 1 1 1 1 1 1 1 1 1 1 1 1 1 1 1 1 1 1 1 1 1 1 1 1 1 1 1 1 1 1 1 1 1 1 1 1 1 1 1 1 1 1 1 1 1 1 1 1 1 1 1 1 1 1 1 1 1 1 1 1
2 2 2 2 2 2 2 2 2 2 2 2 2 2 2 2 2 2 2 2 2 2 2 2 2 2 2 2 2 2 2 2 2 2 2 2 2 2 2 2 2 2 2 2 2 2 2 2 2 2 2 2 2 2 2 2 2 2 2 2 2 2 2 2 2 2 2 2 2 2 2 2 2 2 2 2 2 2 2 2
3 3 3 3 3 3 3 3 3 3 3 3 3 3 3 3 3 3 3 3 3 3 3 3 3 3 3 3 3 3 3 3 3 3 3 3 3 3 3 3 3 3 3 3 3 3 3 3 3 3 3 3 3 3 3 3 3 3 3 3 3 3 3 3 3 3 3 3 3 3 3 3 3 3 3 3 3 3 3 3
4 4 4 4 4 4 4 4 4 4 4 4 4 4 4 4 4 4 4 4 4 4 4 4 4 4 4 4 4 4 4 4 4 4 4 4 4 4 4 4 4 4 4 4 4 4 4 4 4 4 4 4 4 4 4 4 4 4 4 4 4 4 4 4 4 4 4 4 4 4 4 4 4 4 4 4 4 4 4 4
5 5 5 5 5 5 5 5 5 5 5 5 5 5 5 5 5 5 5 5 5 5 5 5 5 5 5 5 5 5 5 5 5 5 5 5 5 5 5 5 5 5 5 5 5 5 5 5 5 5 5 5 5 5 5 5 5 5 5 5 5 5 5 5 5 5 5 5 5 5 5 5 5 5 5 5 5 5 5 5
6 6 6 6 6 6 6 6 6 6 6 6 6 6 6 6 6 6 6 6 6 6 6 6 6 6 6 6 6 6 6 6 6 6 6 6 6 6 6 6 6 6 6 6 6 6 6 6 6 6 6 6 6 6 6 6 6 6 6 6 6 6 6 6 6 6 6 6 6 6 6 6 6 6 6 6 6 6 6 6
7 7 7 7 7 7 7 7 7 7 7 7 7 7 7 7 7 7 7 7 7 7 7 7 7 7 7 7 7 7 7 7 7 7 7 7 7 7 7 7 7 7 7 7 7 7 7 7 7 7 7 7 7 7 7 7 7 7 7 7 7 7 7 7 7 7 7 7 7 7 7 7 7 7 7 7 7 7 7 7
8 8 8 8 8 8 8 8 8 8 8 8 8 8 8 8 8 8 8 8 8 8 8 8 8 8 8 8 8 8 8 8 8 8 8 8 8 8 8 8 8 8 8 8 8 8 8 8 8 8 8 8 8 8 8 8 8 8 8 8 8 8 8 8 8 8 8 8 8 8 8 8 8 8 8 8 8 8 8 8
9 9 9 9 9 9 9 9 9 9 9 9 9 9 9 9 9 9 9 9 9 9 9 9 9 9 9 9 9 9 9 9 9 9 9 9 9 9 9 9 9 9 9 9 9 9 9 9 9 9 9 9 9 9 9 9 9 9 9 9 9 9 9 9 9 9 9 9 9 9 9 9 9 9 9 9 9 9 9 9
1 2 3 4 5 6 7 8 9 10 11 12 13 14 15 16 17 18 19 20 21 22 23 24 25 26 27 28 29 30 31 32 33 34 35 36 37 38 39 40 41 42 43 44 45 46 47 48 49 50 51 52 53 54 55 56 57 58 59 60 61 62 63 64 65 66 67 68 69 70 71 72 73 74 75 76 77 78 79 80
```

Fig. 3. 80-column punched card.

12 rows. In each column a character can be punched, for digits by a hole in the corresponding row number, for letters and other characters by a combination of two or three holes in the same column. At the top of the card space is reserved for the print corresponding to the punch in the columns. The card often has text and layout designed to facilitate punching and other manual handling. A card holds $80 \times 12 = 960$ bits if its entire capacity is used for binary representation. However, the commonly used card codes only utilize a fraction of this. There are a number of different card codes, often depending on national alphabets and wishes for special characters. Further the number of allowed characters is limited. For instance, there are no small letters, which has consequences for card based programming languages. The general confusion with respect to card codes seems partly to have a historical explanation and partly to result from the demand that punched cards should be accessible to treatment by conventional punched cards machines.

Punched paper tape exists in widths between 0.7 and 1 inch and is usually named after the number of channels, i.e. hole positions across the

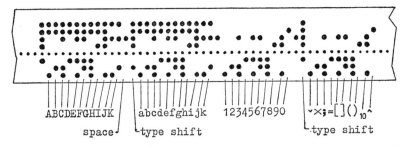

ABCDEFGHIJK   abcdefghijk   1234567890   ⌄×≠=[]()₁₀^
      space⌐   ⌐type shift   ⌐type shift

Fig. 4. 8-channel paper tape.

tape. The narrowest form has 5 channels and is used for binary representation of digits but is also utilized by means of a type shift for a fairly complete representation of digits, letters, and other characters in the international telex code. For a more complete choice of characters, with both capital and small letters, 8-channel tape is used (fig. 4). An 8-channel paper tape of the length 1 foot has roughly the same potential information capacity as a punched card.

2.4. External memories

As mentioned before, the ferrite core memory has a special position as the most frequent internal storage, i.e. the storage where programs and data of immediate interest are stored. However, it is rather expensive and when handling large amounts of data which do not have to be quickly accessible at the same time, it is often sufficient with much slower memory devices. We will here look upon some of the most frequent types, namely drums, disk storages, and magnetic tapes. Usually a distinction is made between sequential storage and random access storage. The former is characterized by the fact that the information is available only in sequence, i.e. it is not possible to treat randomly chosen parts in an economically acceptable way. Thus the parts must be treated only in the order they are placed in the storage. Magnetic tapes are of this type while drums and disks are not.

A *drum memory* consists of a rotating cylinder, the surface of which is covered by a magnetic material. The surface is divided into small parts which can be magnetized in one direction or other and thereby store binary-coded information. The drum rotates at a high speed, 1500—6000 rpm, and the information is read and written by fixed or movable reading and writing heads. The access time depends on the position of the drum at the moment of operation and as an average it is equal to the time for half a revolution, i.e. a few milliseconds. The storing capacity of a drum can reach 10—800 million bits.

The construction of a *disk storage* is characterized by the use of the two sides of metal disks to store information along various tracks, e.g. 100 per side. A movable arm is positioned automatically at the relevant track and the information along it is registered by a reading head, while writing proceeds in an analogous way. A disk storage consists of several, for example 6, disks with arms which can be inserted between the disks like a comb. The choice between the 10 sides (the two outer sides are not used) is made electronically. The disk pack rotates at about 3000 rpm which means an access time of 100 milliseconds. A disk pack of 6 disks in the system described stores about 50 million bits. In some systems the disk packs are easily removable and can be used for storing information off-line.

Magnetic tape is the most used external memory so far and offers an inexpensive and compact form of storage. However, it is a sequential storage requiring a special methodology for rational use. The most common type exists in reels of about 800 yards and is half an inch wide. A reel can hold 50—100 million bits, and information can be transmitted at a speed of 200,000 bits/sec (baud). Magnetic tapes are mounted on tape units where the tape is wound from one reel to another passing reading and writing heads. Magnetic tapes have 7 or 9 channels for information, and data are stored across the tape as with paper tape. Large amounts of data are usually not stored in a continuous sequence on the tape but divided into physical blocks. The block length can be fixed or made dependent on the presence of a block end mark. Between the blocks there is a gap on the tape in order to make it possible for the tape unit to accelerate to full speed between different readings. The selection of block size is decisive of the economy and the treatment in an application with many tape operations. The physical beginning and end of a tape are specially marked. It is common to have strips of aluminum foil for optical recognition. When the tape unit has reached such a mark a signal is given that the unit is ready for action, or has come to the end of the tape. The rewinding of the tape can usually be done both under manual control at the tape unit, and through instructions in the program. In some systems the tape can be read in both directions. There is a special way of avoiding unintentional writing on a tape by use of a metal ring which can be placed on the tape reel.

Mass storages, finally, is a name for memories of random access type which have very large storing capacities (some billion bits) and fairly long access times (0.5—2 secs). They exist in various forms such as large disk storages, magnetic sheets, etc. Intense research and development work is going on within this field.

Chapter 3. Programs and programming languages

Qui vit sans folie n'est pas si sage qu'il le croit.

LA ROCHEFOUCAULD

3.1. Algorithms

e define an *algorithm* as a set of rules which, when carried out, will lead to the solution of a problem in a finite number of steps. An algorithm may concern the computation of square roots of numbers with a desired accuracy. However, the notion of algorithm is not limited to problems of a traditionally mathematical character but contains all types of information processing. Thus, a list of instructions for the placement of words in a word index in their alphabetical order can be regarded as an algorithm.

It is far from trivial to describe the contents of an algorithm in a satisfactory way. This is the case already in communication between human beings where the transmission of information for defining a process often has to take the form of a dialogue to make the definition complete and unique. A written instruction for a tolerably large task will be very extensive and it is difficult to guarantee that no doubts will arise on interpretation.

Of course, our common language with its abundance of words and ambiguity is not a very suitable instrument for the transmission of algorithms to other people or to computers. The mathematical formula language is characterized by its stringency and clarity and must certainly be an integral part of any adequate language for algorithmic description. But the mathematical language is not too well standardized, different mathematicians mean different things with the same symbols, and the symbols often vary in their appearance. Further, there is no developed mathematical language for the handling of parts of quantities, e.g. letters in a word. But the most serious disadvantage is the strongly static tendency in the mathematical language. It aims more at expressing relations and connections and less at expressing actions and changes. The need for dynamics, i.e. the possibility of expressing that something actually has to be executed, must naturally be particularly prominent in an algorithmic language.

19

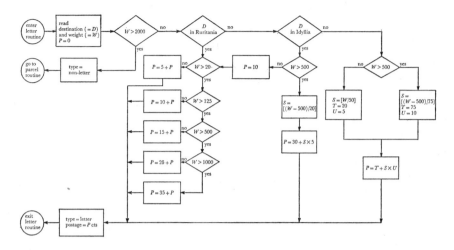

Fig. 5. A flow chart for the computation of Ruritanian letter postage (May, 1928). S, T, U are auxiliary quantities, and P is postage. $[A]$ means here A increased to the nearest higher integer.

We have mentioned the purely verbal way of algorithm description and we have found it unsatisfactory even for human communication. Not least, this form is unsuitable by its inferior surveyability. It is difficult to make a description sufficiently detailed without loosing the general survey of the entire process. A way of solving this problem is the construction of *flow charts* (example in fig. 5). Operations to be performed are specified in boxes, and between these there are connecting lines marked with arrows indicating in which order the different parts of the procedure are supposed to take place. The contents of the boxes can be made as detailed as wanted. In a general survey of the program only the main procedures are indicated. Each of them can then be broken down further into elementary operations in separate detailed flow charts. Attempts have been made at standardizing flow charts and of using well-defined shapes of boxes for the various types of operations to be performed, but still there are no generally accepted standards in this respect.

It is obvious that the methods described for communicating algorithms are unsatisfactory, and even more so if mechanical reading has to be used. The only acceptable method now known is to define formal algorithmic languages. Examples of such languages are ALGOL (Algorithmic Language) and FORTRAN (Formula Translation) which are designed mainly for algorithms of mathematical character. A third example is COBOL, designed to facilitate the formulation of algorithms involving input-output and handling large amounts of data. The degree of computer orientation varies and is much lower in ALGOL than in FORTRAN and COBOL. It is worth noting that algorithmic languages at this level are of utmost importance even through the possibilities they give for the communication of algorithms between humans. However, the connection to computer use is so strong that they are usually called *programming languages*.

3.2. From absolute coding to problem oriented languages

The basic method for the programming of a computer is to write the algorithm, at this stage called the program, in the special code defined for the machine. A particular computer instruction consists of an operation part describing the operation to be performed, e.g. addition, and one or more address parts containing the number of the memory location or locations which will be affected by the operation. In *absolute coding* both these parts are written in exactly the same way as is used by the machine internally. Absolute coding is a severe task from many points of view. For example, the programmer is troubled with many trivial translations and assignments of memory locations. The use of indirect addressing represents a decisive step forward. Then the program is written in such a form that it is not limited to a specific place in the memory but can freely be placed everywhere with the help of a simple loading program which changes the address parts.

Assembly languages will usually allow the writing of programs in alphabetic form. Machine operations are given alphabetic names and the symbols for the used entities can be selected freely. The fairly trivial translation to the number code of the computer and the assigning of memory locations to the entities are managed by a translation program, which also assists with elementary error detection. Most programs written in so-called machine code, are written in this type of languages.

When such machine oriented languages are used, a detailed knowledge of the computer is necessary and the programs produced will be strongly machine dependent. The drawbacks are obvious: the money invested for a large program library or for an integrated data processing system in an enterprise is risked on a possible change of computer. Since technological advances until now has meant that computers will become obsolete after about 5 years use, this is not an insignificant problem. The solution has been the construction of machine independent problem oriented programming languages. The computer manufacturers now furnish special translating programs, *compilers*, along with the hardware. An enterprise having a program library written in languages of this type has become less dependent on a specific manufacturer or a specific machine type.

The term *source program* is often used for a program written in a programming language. *Object program* is the name used for the program which is the result of the translation into machine language. There are two different types of system for running programs written in programming languages. In a *translating system* the whole source program is translated by a special program, the translator or compiler, into an object program which can then be run. The translation may be time-consuming but on the other hand one should expect an efficient object program. In an *interpretive system*, however, the source program instructions are interpreted at execution time. As a rule, this is highly inefficient since the same instructions normally are to be executed several times. In return, interpretive systems are easily constructed which makes it possible to create "private" languages, designed for special problem types and maybe even for a single problem.

3.3. Utilization of computers

A fundamental problem in all data processing is the arrangement of hardware (machine) and software (programs) in such a way as to create a balance between internal and external transmission of information. Even the fastest input-output units have speeds which are much lower than those of the internal units. There are many ways of overcoming these problems and we will mention a few of them. The methods are not exclusive but are usually combined.

A frequent form of organization at large computer installations is to assign the work to different computers. There may be one or several small and fairly slow machines used as satellites to perform the time-consuming input-output operations such as the reading and punching of cards and paper tapes. Information is transmitted to or fetched from magnetic tapes (or other external units). The tapes can then either be manually placed on the tape units of the large computer, or the units can be switched between the satellites and the main computer. In such an arrangement input-output is said to be handled *off-line*; when the central processor of the main computer is directly engaged this is called *on-line*. The organization form with the off-line system is called *batch-processing*, indicating that several programs are collected on tapes via the satellite. They are then executed one by one by the main computer, as a rule under the supervision of a program called the *monitor*. The results are collected on tapes and are printed out later on by the satellites.

In the described mode of action the main computer must still handle the tape units. These fairly slow units, however, are not allowed to block the central processor in fast computers. Usually transmissions between slow memory units and faster ones take place via a separate fast memory called a buffer, or via another part of the central memory. One or more external control units which only have to be initiated by the control unit of the central processor, can handle the transmissions between slow and fast units independently. While these transmissions are going on, the central processor can work with other tasks. In cases when different parts of the central memory are used for different purposes, this takes place under the control of the monitor program.

The trend at the construction of large computers seems to be that satellites for input-output are moved into the central processor both logically and physically. Conversely this can be understood as a development where external control units are becoming more autonomous so that they can handle simple tasks independently.

In this connection we also want to mention the two notions of multiprogramming and time-sharing. *Multiprogramming* is usually reserved for such constructions as the above mentioned with built-in satellite computers where several programs at the same time operate on the same memory. In special cases there are several equal control units which not only operate on the same memory but also on special registers. *Time-sharing* means that the operating system is arranged in such a way that a number of tasks at the same time are kept in the foreground for easy activation. In this way several users can obtain access to the computer simultaneously. Computers with multiprogramming are particularly well suited for such systems, but it is more common that the computer is of ordinary type but with special features for receiving external signals. The running program will then be interrupted and other programs with higher priority activated. Since the machine can easily shift between different tasks, the outward impression is that the computer works on them simultaneously. In such systems a large number of terminals for transmission of data to and from the computer can be attached. Examples of such systems are ticket reservation systems where there are enquiry stations at each sales place and a computer at the central booking office. As the outward activity often does not take more than a fraction of the computer capacity, the machine can also be used in the traditional way by so-called background programs. These will perform routine work on data processing and will be able to run fairly undisturbed as long as they are not interrupted by signals from external units.

Chapter 4. Introduction to COBOL

Если это чай, то я предпочитаю кофе,
а если это кофе, то я желал бы чаю.

4.1. Elements of administrative data processing

he COBOL language is problem oriented and contains means for expressing operations which are typical for administrative or business data processing. One of the main features of COBOL is the standardized way in which it allows large amounts of data to be organized into files, records, and elementary items. We define a *file* to be a set of *records*. Each record describes a certain individual or an event with respect to different properties. When processed on computers files are stored on media of the various types described in Chapter 2, but an ordinary card index, of course, also constitutes a file. File storage media often imply that the records in a file must be treated in sequence. One of the most frequent tasks in this type of file handling is to find a master-file record corresponding to a transaction-file record. The standard technique for solving this problem has been described in Section 1.3.

The basic constituent of a record is the *elementary item*. It is the smallest unit of information which cannot be further divided. Elementary items can be numeric such as numerical identifiers (e.g. numbers) and quantitative measures, or nonnumeric such as alphabetic identifiers (e.g. names) and text.

In a COBOL program files, records, and elementary items are given names which are used for reference. Certain elementary items within a record may be related in such a way that we want to refer to them as a whole. The COBOL language allows the programmer to combine contiguous elementary items into *group items*. For example, the three elementary items month, day, and year may be taken together and form the group item date. Groups, in turn, may be combined into new groups. Hence a hierarchy of relationships between elementary items and group items is established. In the following discussion the term *data item* is used as a general purpose term for an elementary item, a named group of elementary items, or a record.

4.2. History

The decisive step in the direction of creating COBOL was taken in May 1959 at a meeting in the Pentagon in Washington, D.C. Participators at this meeting were representatives from computer users in private industry and government, computer manufacturers, and other interested parties. The purpose was to discuss the need for a general language intended for programming tasks within administrative data processing, and the possibility of creating such a language. The motivation for the meeting was, of course, the fact that the need for such a language in many respects seemed to be evident. As a result a committee was appointed with the name CODASYL (Conference On Data Systems Languages). The committee started to analyze the questions discussed at the meeting, and a subcommittee was entrusted with the direct task of defining a language adapted to administrative data processing. In April 1960 the grammar was published, usually called the report on COBOL-60. This language contained several inadequacies and was soon revised; in 1961 the COBOL-61 report was published. It forms the basis for most current COBOL compilers.

The continued work of the COBOL committee was mostly concerned with following up all activities originating in the report on COBOL-61. Little by little it became obvious that the report contained quite a few vague formulations and even direct contradictions. Further the development of new hardware features demanded new ways of expression which did not exist in COBOL-61. Certain particular problems in typical COBOL applications turned out to be of such a standard character that new and more concentrated notations were developed. All this led to an enlarged COBOL version described in a provisional report "Extended version of COBOL-61" published in 1962. Formally, this meant that a number of new elements were added to the old report.

A completely new report was published by the end of 1965, and this report defines COBOL-65. It contains practically all elements from the "Extended version" but presented in a thoroughly revised form, together with some new elements, mainly devised for expressing the use of random access memories. Although the COBOL-65 version should be sufficient for some years to come, the COBOL committee is still engaged in developing COBOL to keep up with new requirements.

COBOL-65 in its entirety contains so many language elements that it cannot possibly be implemented in full on computers of small or medium size. Therefore it seems reasonable to choose suitable subsets of the language defining them as different standard forms in such a way that the COBOL systems of different computers still become compatible. For COBOL-61 the report suggested two such subsets: REQUIRED and ELECTIVE COBOL. These notions disappeared in COBOL-65, and problems on standardization have been handed over to USASI (United States of America Standards Institute, formerly American Standards Association). In questions of this kind the institute is cooperating with ECMA (European Computer Manufacturers Association) and ISO (International Organization for Standards).

4.3. The structure of a COBOL program

Every COBOL program must be written in four parts, each with its special function. The first part is the *identification division* which is used to identify the program, at least by a name and possibly by remarks under special headings. This part has nothing to do with the work of the computer but must be present in every representation of the program on punched cards or punched tape, in compilation print-outs, and so on.

For every COBOL system the implementor has prescribed the names of the hardware units which may be used by the programmer. In the *environment division* the programmer associates, by using the implementor-names, the hardware units to his own problem-oriented concepts which are then used outside the environment division. For example, a file may be assigned to the card reader in the environment division and when we want to read a card in another part of the program we use our own file-name for reference. The arrangement described makes COBOL almost machine independent and if a program has to be converted from one computer to another, the necessary alterations mainly concern the environment division.

The third part is the *data division*. Here we specify the contents of the files and describe the hierarchy of the data items in the records. We also assign names to the data items and describe them with respect to size, category, decimal point location, and other properties. Finally, working storage and constants are specified as well.

The fourth part is the *procedure division*. This part contains a sequence of statements operating on data specified in the data division. The procedure division is supposed to describe exactly the process for treating data that we want the computer to perform. Depending on the logical structure of the process the statements are collected to paragraphs and, eventually, the paragraphs to sections.

4.4. A simple COBOL program

Before entering upon the details of COBOL we want to show a simple program example. What is remarkable about this program is the fact that it utilizes data material which might be among the oldest on earth, represented in a form which could be called a register. We let the Scriptures speak: "When Adam had lived a hundred and thirty years, he became the father of a son in his own likeness, after his image, and named him Seth. The days of Adam after he became the father of Seth were eight hundred years; and he had other sons and daughters."

Seth was the first ancestor of Noah. For each ancestor of Noah the old Scriptures give information as to name, age on the birth of the next generation, and years of life after this event, in the same way as for Adam. Further it can be derived that Noah was exactly 600 years old when the Flood came, and hence dating of the Flood after the birth of Adam can be seen as a simple data processing problem. We shall now describe this problem by a COBOL program. For each ancestor of Noah the data mentioned above are assumed to form a record, and the records sorted in chronological order are assumed to form a file. In the problem described we only need part of the given information, and in order to use all available information we define one further simple task which can be performed in parallel: the program should also produce a written list with name, birth year, and death year for all ancestors of Noah together with the name and birth year of Noah himself.

Data are to be punched on cards with the following grouping:

Column   1—10 Name
          11—13 Age on birth of next generation
          14—16 Years of life after birth of next generation

The first cards will have the following contents:

```
 0                 1
 1 2 3 4 5 6 7 8 9 0 | 1 2 3 | 4 5 6 | 7                              8
                                                                     0
 ADAM               | 1 3 0 | 8 0 0 |  — — — — — — — — —
 SETH               | 1 0 5 | 8 0 7 |
 ENOS               | 0 9 0 | 8 1 5 |
 .
 .
 .
```

The COBOL program intended to treat these data can be written as follows.

```
IDENTIFICATION DIVISION.
PROGRAM-ID. THE-FLOOD.
AUTHOR. ANNA LYSEGARD.
DATE-WRITTEN. NOV. 4, 1967.

ENVIRONMENT DIVISION.
CONFIGURATION SECTION.
SOURCE-COMPUTER. ABACUS.
OBJECT-COMPUTER. ABACUS.
INPUT-OUTPUT SECTION.
FILE-CONTROL.
    SELECT NOAHS-ANCESTORS ASSIGN TO CARD-READER.
    SELECT LIFELENGTHS ASSIGN TO PRINTER.
```

```
DATA DIVISION.
FILE SECTION.
FD   NOAHS-ANCESTORS
     LABEL RECORDS ARE OMITTED
     DATA RECORD IS ANCESTOR.
01   ANCESTOR.
     02 NAME PICTURE A(10).
     02 AGE-1 PICTURE 999.
     02 TIME-2 PICTURE 999.
FD   LIFELENGTHS
     LABEL RECORDS ARE OMITTED
     DATA RECORD IS TEXT.
01   TEXT.
     02 NAME-OUT PICTURE A(10).
     02 BIRTH-YEAR PICTURE Z(8).
     02 DEATH-YEAR PICTURE Z(8).
WORKING-STORAGE SECTION.
77   TIME-AFTER-ADAM PICTURE 9999 VALUE IS ZERO.

PROCEDURE DIVISION.
START.  OPEN INPUT NOAHS-ANCESTORS
        OUTPUT LIFELENGTHS.
READ-RECORD.  READ NOAHS-ANCESTORS
     AT END GO TO TERMINATION.
     MOVE NAME TO NAME-OUT.
     MOVE TIME-AFTER-ADAM TO BIRTH-YEAR.
     ADD AGE-1 TO TIME-AFTER-ADAM.
     ADD TIME-AFTER-ADAM AND TIME-2 GIVING
     DEATH-YEAR.
     WRITE TEXT. GO TO READ-RECORD.
TERMINATION.  CLOSE NOAHS-ANCESTORS.
     MOVE "NOAH" TO NAME-OUT.
     MOVE TIME-AFTER-ADAM TO BIRTH-YEAR.
     MOVE ZERO TO DEATH-YEAR.
     WRITE TEXT. CLOSE LIFELENGTHS.
     ADD 600 TO TIME-AFTER-ADAM.
     DISPLAY "THE FLOOD CAME IN YEAR",
     TIME-AFTER-ADAM. STOP RUN.
```

Formally the program is a sequence of headings and sentences constructed by the aid of key words with special significance and of problem oriented concepts created by the programmer. As a rule, the meaning of the key words is intuitively clear, and a thorough knowledge of the COBOL grammar should not be necessary for a reasonable understanding of a COBOL program. We will now give a general outline of the program above.

The program starts with IDENTIFICATION DIVISION which is a fixed heading of the corresponding part of the program. Except for the program name which must not be left out, this program is identified by the author name and construction date.

In the ENVIRONMENT DIVISION the computer installation is first described in general terms under the header CONFIGURATION SECTION; our program will be both compiled and run on the computer ABACUS. In the INPUT-OUTPUT SECTION the file NOAHS-ANCESTORS is linked to the card-reader of the computer. The list which will be written out is also considered as a file. It has the name LIFELENGTHS and is linked to the printer of the computer.

In the DATA DIVISION the files and their records are described in the FILE SECTION. Concerning the file NOAHS – ANCESTORS we are first told that it is not provided with any special characteristics, and that it contains one type of records with the name ANCESTOR. The contents of such a record are then described; it contains three elementary items NAME, AGE – 1, and TIME – 2. The contents of the elementary items are visualized in a PICTURE, one for each item. NAME is a sequence of 10 alphabetic characters (including spaces) which is symbolized by A(10), while AGE – 1 and TIME – 2 are three-digit integers which is symbolized by 999. We note that the record description has a direct counterpart in the field formats of the punched cards. Also the file LIFELENGTHS is not provided with special characteristics. Here every record corresponds to a line in the written list and contains three elementary items NAME – OUT, BIRTH – YEAR, and DEATH – YEAR. NAME – OUT is a sequence of 10 alphabetic characters (including spaces). BIRTH – YEAR and DEATH – YEAR occupy 8 positions each in the line. The symbol Z indicates that when a number is stored in the area of the corresponding elementary item, any leading zeros in the number are to be automatically replaced by blanks. The second part of the data division is the WORKING – STORAGE SECTION which specifies necessary working-area in the internal storage of the computer. In our case we need an auxiliary variable TIME – AFTER – ADAM used on computation of birth years. Before the computer starts executing the program the value zero is assigned to this variable.

The PROCEDURE DIVISION has been written in three paragraphs. The paragraph START has the effect that the file NOAHS – ANCESTORS is opened for reading and the file LIFELENGTHS is opened for writing. In this way the card reader is prepared to read cards and the printer to print the output. In the paragraph READ – RECORD all records from the file NOAHS – ANCESTORS are read one by one until the file has been scanned. On reading, the contents of the record are placed in a special storage area which has been assigned to the file and the contents are now available for e.g. arithmetic operations and internal transfers. A similar area has been reserved for the output file. To this area we transfer the ancestor's name and the value of TIME – AFTER – ADAM which is the birth year of the ancestor under consideration. The value of DEATH – YEAR is computed and transferred to the same area, and finally the whole record is written out. Simultaneously TIME – AFTER – ADAM has been updated. When the input file contains no more records the paragraph TERMINATION is performed. The input file is closed and disconnected from the input-output system. The data for NOAH are written out as a last record on the list as soon as the character string "NOAH" has been stored in NAME – OUT, the value of TIME – AFTER – ADAM in BIRTH – YEAR, and blanks in DEATH – YEAR. After that the output file is also closed. Finally, the number 600 is added

to Noah's birth year and the result is written out preceded by the text
"THE FLOOD CAME IN YEAR". This last print-out will appear on the
unit which is standard for reporting to the operator while the computer is
running. This concludes the program, and STOP RUN will signal the end
of the program so that the computer may proceed to the next job.

4.5. Characters

All language elements of COBOL are formed by use of the following 51
characters:

0 1 2 3 4 5 6 7 8 9	digits
A B C D E F G H I J K L M	letters
N O P Q R S T U V W X Y Z	
	blank
+	plus sign
–	minus sign or hyphen
*	multiplication sign or asterisk
/	division sign
=	equal sign
$	dollar sign (currency sign)
,	comma
;	semicolon
.	period or decimal point
"	quotation mark
(	left parenthesis
)	right parenthesis
>	greater than
<	less than

Depending on the function the symbols are assigned to different categories,
sometimes to several categories simultaneously:

Characters for forming words: digits, letters, and hyphen
Characters for punctuation: , ; . " ( ) and blank
Characters for arithmetic: + – * / =
Characters for forming relations: = > <
Editing symbols: B 0 + – CR DB Z * $, .

From a typographic point of view blanks have a special position. In
ordinary text they are represented just as spaces between characters of
other kinds. Since blanks have an essential function in COBOL we must
write all symbols in assumed or actual columns in such a way that in the

same line each column contains exactly one symbol. In Section 4.8. we shall discuss this problem in more detail.

A COBOL program consists of a sequence of words and literals whose relationship is indicated by the symbols for punctuation, arithmetic, and relations.

4.6. Words

Formally a *word* consists of not more than 30 characters, digits, letters, and hyphens. However, a word must not begin or end with a hyphen. The end of a word is indicated with a following blank or right parenthesis, or with a period, comma, or semicolon which must then be followed by a blank. After such a separator an arbitrary number of blanks is allowed. These rules imply that a blank cannot appear inside a word.

The words may be *reserved words* or *names*. All words appearing in formats in the COBOL report are reserved; the total number of such reserved COBOL words is 284.[1] From the user's point of view the so-called *implementor-names*[2] are also reserved words. These words are fixed by the constructor of a certain COBOL system, and they are used as names for different units in the special computer installation. The reserved words are of two kinds: *key words* which are of real significance for the contents of the program, and *optional words* which may be inserted at will in certain constructions. The optional words have no effect on the function of a program but are justified by increased readability. Among the key words the *verbs* are used for ordering a part of the procedure division to be executed, e.g. ADD, READ, ENTER.

Names are formed by the programmer. Of course, they must not be identical with any of the reserved words. Names may stand for different concepts, and in these respects there are certain restrictions for their construction. *Data-names* are used for files and data items which are described in the data division. These words must contain at least one alphabetic character, e.g. ALPHA, 4X4, R – 2. *Condition-names* are formed in the same way as data-names and stand for logical variables which can have the values true or false. A condition-name is associated on one hand to a certain data item, on the other to a set of values which can be assumed by this data item. If on some occasion the value of the data item belongs to this set, then the value of the condition is true, otherwise false. Condition-names offer good opportunities of testing relations in a concise way. How the association is performed will be described in Chapter 9. *Procedure-names* designate paragraphs or sections. A procedure-name does not neces-

---

[1] A list of the reserved COBOL words can be found at the end of this book (p. 138).
[2] In the COBOL-61 report the term hardware-name was used instead of implementor-name.

sarily have to contain an alphabetic character but may consist of just digits. It should be observed that such names are equal only if they are composed of the same digits in the same order; hence the number of digits must also be the same. For example, 0081, 081, and 81 are different procedure-names. *Mnemonic names* are formed in the same way as data-names. In the environment division they are connected to implementor-names, and in other parts of the program they function as symbolic names of corresponding hardware units. If we want to move a program from one computer to another with the same capacity but with different external units, the necessary changes affect only the environment division.

4.7. Literals

A *literal* is defined as a string of characters whose value is implied by the set of characters comprising the string. There are two types of literals, numeric and nonnumeric. They are separated from other elements in a program according to the same rules as are valid for words. *Numeric literals* are represented essentially in the same way as in mathematics: 67, 0, -10000, 2.453, -173.50, and so on. We can write $+1.2$ or 1.2, and both stand for the same value; also 0.34 and .34 designate the same value. The use of more than one plus or minus sign is not allowed and the sign must appear as the leftmost character of the literal. The form 2. is not accepted; we have to write either 2 or 2.0, possibly with a plus sign. The two alternatives represent the same value, but under certain circumstances only the first alternative is allowed since it has the form of an integer. *Integers* are defined as numeric literals whose representation does not contain a decimal point.

A *nonnumeric literal* is a string of symbols, all COBOL characters except " being allowed everywhere in the sequence. In the COBOL program the literal represents itself, i.e. the character string, but it must begin and end with a quotation mark to be distinguishable from e.g. data-names. It should be observed that blanks inside the quotation marks are treated exactly in the same way as other symbols and enter as parts of the literal. Character strings forming reserved words may, of course, also be present in non-numeric literals. Examples of nonnumeric literals are "EXAMINE CLOCK NUMBER", "PAGE 144 MISSING", and "-125.65". The character sequence in the last example must be distinguished from the number -125.65 which is a numeric literal.

For certain literals with special meaning alternative notations forming COBOL words, so-called *figurative constants*, have been reserved. Some of them will be mentioned here. The word ZERO represents the value 0 or one or several symbols 0 depending on the context. Instead of ZERO we can write ZEROS, or ZEROES. The word SPACE can be used for representing one or several blanks. Instead of SPACE we can also write SPACES. The word QUOTE (or QUOTES) represents one or several quotation marks. By that we can also handle this character in a COBOL program in spite of the fact that the symbol " must not appear in a literal. The possibility with QUOTE is utilized when we want a data item to contain quotation marks or when we want a print-out of such a character (see examples in 5.7.). The COBOL word ALL followed by a nonnumeric literal represents one or several sets of the character sequence which the literal contains. We give the examples ALL "9", ALL "ABC", ALL ZEROS. The last example is a correct construction, but it has the same meaning as ZEROS alone. The figurative constants are used mainly in storing operations when we want to fill a data item with symbols of the same kind.

4.8. Formats and reference format

When we describe the constituents of a COBOL program in the following chapters, we shall make frequent use of so-called *formats*. Such a format will indicate allowed combinations of words, literals, and special symbols in a statement by use of a uniform symbolism. As an example we consider a format for multiplication:

$$\underline{\text{MULTIPLY}} \left\{ \begin{array}{l} \text{identifier-1} \\ \text{literal-1} \end{array} \right\} \underline{\text{BY}}\ \text{identifier-2}\ [\underline{\text{ROUNDED}}]$$

[, identifier-3 [ROUNDED]] ... [; ON SIZE ERROR imperative-statement]

All words in capitals are reserved COBOL words. Key words are under-lined while optional words are not. Words in small letters are generic terms and represent COBOL words which are to be supplied by the pro-grammer. The term *identifier* is a common word for data-names, qualified data-names (described in 6.2.), and subscripted data-names (described in 6.6.).[1] If several generic terms of the same kind are present in a format, then, as a rule, they are specified by a following digit in order to simplify identification when the format is discussed.

If a certain part of a format is enclosed within brackets, [ ], this indicates that the part in question is optional. If there are several alternatives inside the brackets, these alternatives are placed on top of each other. If a certain part is enclosed by braces, { }, this means that one of the alternatives within the braces must be chosen. Three points, ..., always preceded by] or } indicate that the concept before the points may be repeated an arbitrary number of times.

[1] In COBOL-61 the term data-name was used also for identifiers which made certain formats hard to describe. This terminology is still used in several manuals.

A *comma* in a format is always optional and may be included or omitted by the programmer. It is used to separate operands, e.g. identifiers or literals, in order to improve the readability of the program. There are two additional options with the same effect, viz. the COBOL word AND and comma followed by AND. For example, the four constructions

```
MULTIPLY A BY B C
MULTIPLY A BY B , C
MULTIPLY A BY B AND C
MULTIPLY A BY B , AND C
```

are completely equivalent. In a similar way we have sequences of statements and clauses separated by *semicolon* which can be left out without changing the meaning.

Starting from the format above we give some further examples of COBOL statements for multiplication:

```
MULTIPLY A BY B
MULTIPLY 1.2 BY C ROUNDED
MULTIPLY -1000 BY D ON SIZE ERROR GO TO L1
MULTIPLY R1 BY R2 , R3 ROUNDED , R4 , R5 ;
SIZE ERROR GO TO ERROR-ROUTINE
```

The exact meaning of these statements will be explained in Section 5.4.

In order to give all COBOL programs a uniform shape the COBOL report stipulates that the *reference format* must be obeyed. In Section 4.5. we pointed out that when one writes a COBOL program every character must occupy one position. In practice, the writing must be divided into several lines, all lines having the same number of positions. For every input or output medium, the compiler constructor must specify what is meant by lines and positions. The reference format means that for one line, independently of the medium, a number of margins has been introduced. The location of such a margin is given by the distance in number of positions from the first position of the line, the *left margin*. The representation of different elements in the program must start at certain fixed margins.

The first six positions are reserved for a *sequence number* with respect to the lines. In practice this is usually divided into a three-digit page number and a three-digit line number. Often we write the line numbers as 010, 020, 030, and so on which gives us an opportunity to insert up to nine extra lines when correcting the program, and still maintain an ascending number sequence. Position 7 represents a continuation area and corresponds to the *C-margin*. Here we place a hyphen if the last word in the preceding line must be terminated in the new line. Position 8 corresponds to the *A-margin*; here all elements of the program with a heading function are started, e.g. fixed headings and paragraph-names. Position 12 corresponds

34

System	ABACUS			Punching Instructions			Sheet 2 of 3
Program	THE-FLOOD		Graphic			Card Form # *	Identification
Programmer	ANNA LYSEGARD	Date 11.04.67	Punch				73] [80

```
SEQUENCE
(PAGE)(SERIAL)  A    B
  3  4  6  7 8  12  16  20  24  28  32  36  40  44  48  52  56  60  64  68  72
0020 10  DATA DIVISION.
    020  FILE SECTION.
    030  FD  NØAHS-ANCESTØRS.
    040      LABEL RECØRDS ARE ØMITTED
    050      DATA RECØRD IS ANCESTØR.
    060  01  ANCESTØR.
    070      02 NAME PICTURE A(10).
    080      02 AGE-1 PICTURE 999.
    090      02 TIME-2 PICTURE 999.
    100  FD  LIFELENGTHS
    110      LABEL RECØRDS ARE ØMITTED
    120      DATA RECØRD IS TEXT.
    130  01  TEXT.
    140      02 NAME-ØUT PICTURE A(10).
    150      02 BIRTH-YEAR PICTURE Z(8).
    160      02 DEATH-YEAR PICTURE Z(8).
    170  WØRKING-STØRAGE SECTIØN.
    180  77  TIME-AFTER-ADAM PICTURE 9999 VALUE IS ZERØ.
```

*A standard card form, IBM electro C61897, is available for punching source statements from this form.

Fig. 6. Coding sheet for representing COBOL programs on punched cards. Each line on the sheet corresponds to one card.

to the *B-margin* where normally each new line will begin. The last position of the line defines a *right margin*. The reference format is illustrated in the following figure:

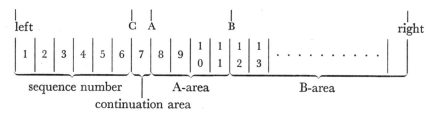

In practice, COBOL programs are usually written on special forms devised with regard to the reference format and a line length depending on the input medium. The forms can then be used directly when the program is punched. An example of such a coding form is shown in fig. 6.

Exercises

1. Which of the following notations are legitimate as data-names and procedure-names respectively?

a) ADAM   b) DC31   c) PI –   d) ENTER   e) 14

f) 22 – K   g) RIGHT   h) P(J)   i) A – B – C   j) 1 – 1

2. Which of the following strings denote numeric literals?

a) +1   b) 1,01   c) –.12   d) 24.12.65   e) 383.

f) 0.12   g) "48.30"   h) – 36EE – 1 i) – 02

3. Below follows the procedure division of a COBOL program which computes the sum of the integers 1, 2, 3, ... up to 100. Using intuition, find a) the COBOL words, b) the data-names, c) the procedure-names, and d) the numeric literals.

```
INIT. MOVE ZERO TO K, TOTAL.
NEW-K. ADD 1 TO K ADD K TO TOTAL
     IF K IS LESS THAN 100 GO TO NEW-K.
TERMINATION. DISPLAY TOTAL STOP RUN.
```

Chapter 5. The procedure division

"... and then I disconnected the booster from the Electro-Snuggie Blanket and put him in the deep-freeze. In the morning I defrosted him and ran him through the Handi Home Slicer and then the Jiffy Burger Grind, and after that I fed him down the Dispose-All. Then I washed my clothes in the Bendix, tidied up the kitchen, and went to a movie."

CHAS. ADDAMS

5.1. Introduction

n this chapter we consider the part that is placed last in a COBOL program, viz. the *procedure division*. The procedure division describes the processing to be performed on the data items defined in a previous part, the data division. The processing can be of several different kinds: input, output, transfers, arithmetic operations, and so on.

The procedure division is headed by PROCEDURE DIVISION and is written as a sequence of *statements*. A statement begins with a key word, the *verb*, which tells what is going to happen, and after this come the data involved, and possibly words which modify the action of the verb. Example:

```
ADD 1 TO TOTAL
```

This is a statement where ADD is the verb while 1 is a numeric literal and TOTAL a name. Both refer to data affected by the verb, while TO is a word modifying the action of ADD. The result of the statement is that the value of TOTAL is increased by 1. Using another modification word we can assign a different action to the verb ADD. Our discussion of the procedure division in the following sections will consist of an enumeration of a set of important verbs, a definition of their formats, and a description of how they are used.

One or several statements together, terminated by a period followed by a space form a *sentence*. Example:

```
ADD 1 TO A   GO TO READY.
```
   statement   statement

Every sentence must belong to a *paragraph*. A paragraph has a name which is written starting at the A-margin. The name must be followed by a period and a space. After the paragraph-name we have the sentences which are not allowed to start to the left of the B-margin. Examples:

37

```
SUMMATION.  ADD X TO SUM-1.
     ADD 1 TO TOTAL.  GO TO READY.
P1.  DISPLAY TOTAL.
```

The first paragraph has the name SUMMATION and contains three sentences; the second has the name P1 and contains only one sentence. It is possible to combine all the paragraphs into *sections* which is often convenient in large programs. A section contains one or more paragraphs preceded by a *section header* consisting of a section-name followed by the word SECTION and a period. The section header is written on a line of its own beginning at the A-margin. Example:

```
FINAL-COMPUTATION SECTION.
SUMMATION.  ADD X TO SUM-1.
     ADD 1 TO TOTAL.
WRITE-OUT.  DISPLAY SUM-1.
     DISPLAY TOTAL.
```

The section FINAL-COMPUTATION consists of the two paragraphs SUMMATION and WRITE-OUT.

5.2. Representation of data

Before we can describe how processing of data is performed in COBOL, we must briefly comment on how they are represented in the computer. Every data item is described in the data division and is in this way classified as numeric, alphabetic, or alphanumeric. An alphanumeric elementary item is characterized by the fact that it may contain arbitrary characters. Moreover, the size of the item, which is the number of characters, is also given in the data division. For numeric elementary items we can further specify the location of the decimal point and whether both positive and negative values may be assigned to the item. If the decimal point specification is missing, the item is considered as an integer, and if the sign specification is missing, the item can only contain positive numbers or zero. Numeric items are supposed to occupy as much space in the computer as corresponds to the maximum number of decimal digits the item can contain; possibly occurring plus- or minus-signs and decimal point are controlled by the computer in some other way. Literals of different kinds are specified through their appearance and are stored in the same manner as data items. On arithmetic operations the decimal point is automatically placed in its correct position. If, for example, A stands for a five-digit elementary item with two decimals, and the area reserved for A contains 04711, then A has the value 47.11. If the number 3, stored in a one-digit area, is added to A, then the area occupied by A will contain 05011 which means that the value 50.11 has been assigned to A. In order to indicate that the assumed decimal point does not occupy a character position but still has influence on the value of a numeric item, we shall henceforth use a caret to show its place, e.g. 050₁1.

5.3. Transfers

When we want to transfer information from one place in the internal storage to another we can use the verb MOVE. It has the format:

$$\underline{\text{MOVE}} \left\{ \begin{array}{l} \text{identifier-1} \\ \text{literal} \end{array} \right\} \underline{\text{TO}} \text{ identifier-2 [, identifier-3]} \ldots$$

The points indicate that the same information can be transferred to several different places with the same MOVE-statement. Examples:

```
MOVE   1 0   TO   TOTAL
MOVE   SUM- 1   TO   RESULT
MOVE   ZERO   TO   I ,   J ,   K
MOVE   "DAY-REPORT"   TO   NAME
MOVE   ALL   " * "   TO   SYMB-SEQUENCE
```

After the MOVE-statement has been performed, the receiving area has the same contents as the transmitting area if the data description entries coincide. If they differ, the assumed decimal points on transfer of numeric items are automatically adapted, and if necessary, zeros are inserted or superfluous decimals eliminated when the data are stored. On transfer of nonnumeric items they are stored character by character from left to right into the receiving area. If necessary, spaces are filled in or superfluous characters eliminated. In Chapter 6 we shall discuss the result of transfers in more detail and examine how it is influenced by different descriptions of the data items. It should be observed that the contents of the transmitting area are not destroyed or changed in any way through a MOVE-statement.

5.4. Arithmetic

We are now going to describe how numerical computations are performed in COBOL. At our disposal we have the verbs ADD, SUBTRACT, MULTIPLY, and DIVIDE for the four simple rules of arithmetic. However, there is also a more general verb, COMPUTE, which can conveniently be used when more complicated expressions have to be computed. The quantities which enter a computation can be numeric literals as well as identifiers to which values have been assigned previously in the program. The result of a computation is always a numerical value which will be assigned to an identifier.

ADD is the verb which is used for addition. There are three different ways in which it may be applied as is demonstrated in the following formats:

$$1) \quad \underline{\text{ADD}} \left\{ \begin{array}{l} \text{identifier-1} \\ \text{literal-1} \end{array} \right\} \left[\begin{array}{l} , \text{ identifier-2} \\ , \text{ literal-2} \end{array} \right] \ldots, \text{ identifier-}n$$

2) $\underline{\text{ADD}} \left\{ \begin{array}{l} \text{identifier-1} \\ \text{literal-1} \end{array} \right\} \left[\begin{array}{l} \text{, identifier-2} \\ \text{, literal-2} \end{array} \right] \dots$

   $\underline{\text{TO}}$ identifier-m [, identifier-n] ...

3) $\underline{\text{ADD}} \left\{ \begin{array}{l} \text{identifier-1} \\ \text{literal-1} \end{array} \right\}, \left\{ \begin{array}{l} \text{identifier-2} \\ \text{literal-2} \end{array} \right\} \left[\begin{array}{l} \text{, identifier-3} \\ \text{, literal-3} \end{array} \right] \dots$

   $\underline{\text{GIVING}}$ identifier-m [, identifier-n] ...

When the first format is used, the values of all operands are added and the result is stored into the storage area denoted by identifier-n, while all other areas are left unchanged. In format 2 the values of all operands coming before TO are added, and this sum is then added to each identifier coming after TO, the results being stored in the areas reserved for these identifiers. The third format causes the values of all operands before GIVING to be added, and the result to be stored in the storage areas denoted by identifier-m, identifier-n, and so on.

The verb SUBTRACT has two formats:

1) $\underline{\text{SUBTRACT}} \left\{ \begin{array}{l} \text{identifier-1} \\ \text{literal-1} \end{array} \right\} \left[\begin{array}{l} \text{, identifier-2} \\ \text{, literal-2} \end{array} \right] \dots$

   $\underline{\text{FROM}}$ identifier-m [, identifier-n] ...

2) $\underline{\text{SUBTRACT}} \left\{ \begin{array}{l} \text{identifier-1} \\ \text{literal-1} \end{array} \right\} \left[\begin{array}{l} \text{, identifier-2} \\ \text{, literal-2} \end{array} \right] \dots$

   $\underline{\text{FROM}} \left\{ \begin{array}{l} \text{identifier-}m \\ \text{literal-}m \end{array} \right\} \underline{\text{GIVING}}$ identifier-n [, identifier-o] ...

If the first format is used the values of the operands before FROM are added and then the sum is subtracted from the value of identifier-m, identifier-n, and so on, the different results being stored in the corresponding areas. In the second case the values of the operands before FROM are also added, the sum then being subtracted from identifier-m (literal-m) and the result placed into the areas for identifier-n, identifier-o, and so on.

The verb MULTIPLY also has two formats:

1) $\underline{\text{MULTIPLY}} \left\{ \begin{array}{l} \text{identifier-1} \\ \text{literal-1} \end{array} \right\} \underline{\text{BY}}$ identifier-2 [, identifier-3] ...

2) $\underline{\text{MULTIPLY}} \left\{ \begin{array}{l} \text{identifier-1} \\ \text{literal-1} \end{array} \right\} \underline{\text{BY}} \left\{ \begin{array}{l} \text{identifier-2} \\ \text{literal-2} \end{array} \right\}$

   $\underline{\text{GIVING}}$ identifier-3 [, identifier-4] ...

With the first format the value of each identifier after BY is multiplied by the value of the operand before BY and the result stored in the area reserved for the identifier after BY. With the second format the product of the first two operands is assigned to identifier-3, identifier-4, and so on.

For the verb DIVIDE, finally, there are three options:

1) DIVIDE $\left\{ \begin{array}{l} \text{identifier-1} \\ \text{literal-1} \end{array} \right\}$ INTO identifier-2 [, identifier-3] ...

2) DIVIDE $\left\{ \begin{array}{l} \text{identifier-1} \\ \text{literal-1} \end{array} \right\}$ INTO $\left\{ \begin{array}{l} \text{identifier-2} \\ \text{literal-2} \end{array} \right\}$

   GIVING identifier-3 [, identifier-4] ...

3) DIVIDE $\left\{ \begin{array}{l} \text{identifier-1} \\ \text{literal-1} \end{array} \right\}$ BY $\left\{ \begin{array}{l} \text{identifier-2} \\ \text{literal-2} \end{array} \right\}$

   GIVING identifier-3 [, identifier-4] ...

If we use the first format the value of each identifier after INTO is divided by the value of the operand before INTO and the result stored in the area reserved for the identifier after INTO. With the second format the value obtained when the second operand is divided by the first is assigned to identifier-3, identifier-4, and so on. With the third format, finally, the first operand is divided by the second, the value obtained being assigned to all identifiers after GIVING.

We here present a table showing the results of statements containing the verbs ADD, SUBTRACT, MULTIPLY, and DIVIDE.

Variable:	A	B	C	D	E
Value before execution:	5	15	8	−3	12
Value after execution of:					
ADD C E			8		20
ADD A B C D	5	15	8	25	
ADD 3 A A	13				
ADD A TO B	5	20			
ADD A D TO E	5			−3	14
ADD A B TO C D	5	15	28	17	
ADD A B GIVING C	5	15	20		
ADD −8 C GIVING D			8	0	
ADD C D GIVING B D E		5	8	5	5
SUBTRACT A FROM B	5	10			
SUBTRACT A C FROM A D E	−8		8	−16	−1
SUBTRACT E 2 FROM B GIVING D		15		1	12
MULTIPLY A BY B	5	75			
MULTIPLY 3 BY A D	15			−9	
MULTIPLY A BY B GIVING D	5	15		75	
DIVIDE A INTO B	5	3			
DIVIDE 4 INTO C E			2		3
DIVIDE 3 INTO 90 GIVING D				30	
DIVIDE 150 BY B GIVING A B	10	10			

However, if we want to perform more complicated computations, the simple arithmetic verbs soon become unwieldy. In such situations the verb COMPUTE offers much better possibilities to describe the desired computations in a clear and comprehensive way. This verb has the format:

$$\underline{\text{COMPUTE}} \text{ identifier-1 [, identifier-2]} \ldots \begin{Bmatrix} \text{FROM} \\ = \\ \text{EQUALS} \end{Bmatrix} \begin{Bmatrix} \text{identifier-}n \\ \text{literal} \\ \text{arithmetic-expression} \end{Bmatrix}$$

The effect of such a statement is that the value represented within the last braces is computed and assigned to the identifiers before the symbol = (or FROM or EQUALS, which are all equivalent). An *arithmetic expression* is written in about the same way as in ordinary mathematics by use of identifiers, numeric literals, arithmetic operators, and parentheses. The symbols for the different operations are:

+   addition
−   subtraction
*   multiplication
/   division
**   exponentiation (raised to the power of)

It should be mentioned that these arithmetic operators may be replaced by equivalent COBOL-words: PLUS, MINUS, TIMES or MULTIPLIED BY, DIVIDED BY, and EXPONENTIATED BY. When an arithmetic expression is evaluated, operations within parentheses are executed first, then exponentiation, then multiplication and division, and finally addition and subtraction. Thus it is not necessary to use parentheses more often than usual. It should be observed that the multiplication symbol must not be omitted as is common in mathematical formula language. Further, a blank must surround all arithmetic operators (but not the leading + or − in a numeric literal); however, a blank must not follow a left parenthesis, nor is a blank allowed to precede a right parenthesis. Examples:

```
COMPUTE  A  =  B  +  C
COMPUTE  D  =  X  **  2  -  Y  **  2
COMPUTE  OVERTIME  =  HOURLY-WAGE  *  1.5  *  (TIME  -  40)
COMPUTE  DISTANCE  =  PLACE-1  -  PLACE-2
COMPUTE  VELOCITY  =  DISTANCE  /  TIME
COMPUTE  S  =  18  /  (T  +  (S  +  T  *  3)  **  2)
COMPUTE  T,  Y,  Z  =  -5.2  *  (T  +  Z)  *  (T  +  Y)
```

It sometimes happens that a computed result has more decimals than are available in the area where it will be stored. In such cases the last decimals in the result are automatically eliminated. Example:

42

If   A   0 4 1 2̬ 6

and   B   2 6̬   then the statement ADD A B GIVING C

yields   C   0 4 3 8̬

The true result of the addition is 43.86, but since C can accomodate just one decimal the last digit disappears when the number is stored. If we desire the result to be *rounded* before it is stored, this is indicated by use of the word ROUNDED after the proper identifier. Example:

If   A   0 4 1 2̬ 6

and   B   2 6̬   then the statement

                ADD A B GIVING C ROUNDED D E ROUNDED

yields   C   0 4 3 9̬

        D   4 3̬

        E   4 3 8̬ 6 0

The usual rounding rules are applied, and in case C we get the result 43.9 since the first neglected digit is 5 or more. Since E has space for three decimals, no change of the result takes place. We give one further example:

COMPUTE CIRCUMFERENCE ROUNDED = 3.1416 * DIAMETER

If   DIAMETER   0 1 2 1̬

then CIRCUMFERENCE 0 0 3 8 0̬ 1 3

The result of the multiplication is 38.01336 which is rounded to 38.013.

If the programmer is not careful the area reserved for an identifier may not be sufficient to store the result of an operation. If, for example, A has a three-digit area and the value 689, then the statement ADD 500 TO A gives a value 1189 which is too large to be stored in the area for A. As a matter of fact, the value of A after such an operation is undefined. In order to avoid programming errors it is highly important that the programmer makes sure that sufficient space is reserved for all identifiers when a COBOL program is constructed. However, it is sometimes impossible to predict their sizes, but COBOL then offers a possibility for control when the program is executed. This is done by adding the following phrase to the arithmetic statement.

; ON SIZE ERROR imperative-statement

Imperative-statement stands for those statements which follow until the end of the sentence. None of these statements is allowed to begin with IF (see 5.6.) or READ (see 5.7.), or to contain another SIZE ERROR-element. The statements in the sentence are performed as soon as the result of the computation has become too large to be stored in anyone of the receiving areas. The corresponding identifier keeps its old value while the storing proceeds as usual for other identifiers if such are present. Examples:

```
ADD 100 TO TIME ON SIZE ERROR MOVE 9999 TO TIME
GO TO ERROR-ROUTINE.
MULTIPLY LENGTH-1 BY LENGTH-2 GIVING AREA-1
ON SIZE ERROR MOVE ZERO TO AREA-1.
```

5.5. Flow control

The normal sequence of execution is for a computer to process the statements in a program one after the other from the first to the last. The great usefulness of the computer, however, is based on its ability to interrupt the sequential execution flow and repeat the same part over and over or to switch to a different part of the program. The programmer has to decide how and under what conditions the computer must modify its operations, depending upon the data encountered or the results of the computations.

In this section we shall describe the verbs GO, PERFORM, and STOP, all of which interrupt the normal sequential execution of statements as written in the program. Further, in Section 5.6. we shall treat IF-statements which can be used when we want the computer to modify its action according to certain conditions.

If an interruption is desired of the sequential execution of the statements in the procedure division, then a statement containing the verb GO can be used. It has the format:

GO TO procedure-name

In the following we are going to use the *procedure* concept in order to indicate a certain piece of program which may consist of one or several paragraphs or sections. In the format above procedure-name stands for the paragraph or section to the beginning of which a jump should be performed. After the jump the statements of the procedure are performed one by one until possibly another jump causes a new interrupt. Example:

GO TO WRITE-OUT-PART

There is also a possibility to give the computer alternative routes to be chosen under the control of the value of an identifier which can only take integer values. In this case we make use of a GO-statement with the format:

GO TO procedure-name-1 [, procedure-name-2] ... , procedure-name-n
    DEPENDING ON identifier

If the value of the identifier is 1, a jump is performed to procedure-name-1, if the value is 2, a jump is performed to procedure-name-2, and so on. However, if the value is zero, or negative or greater than the number of procedure-names, the statement has no effect, and instead the next statement in the procedure division is performed. Example:

GO TO MALE FEMALE DEPENDING ON SEX

Sometimes we want to execute a number of statements in some other part of the procedure division and then return. In such cases the verb PERFORM can be applied. In its simplest form it has the following format.

PERFORM procedure-name-1 [THRU procedure-name-2]

The COBOL word THRU may be replaced by THROUGH which is completely equivalent. Exactly as is the case with GO, the procedure-names in the format correspond to names of paragraphs or sections. A PERFORM-statement has the following effect. A jump is performed to the first statement of the procedure symbolized by procedure-name-1, and this and subsequent statements are executed. If procedure-name-2 is not specified, a return jump is automatically made after completion of the last sentence of procedure-name-1 to the statement following the PERFORM-statement; otherwise the return is after the last sentence of procedure-name-2. Examples:

PERFORM READ-IN
PERFORM IN-DATA THRU WRITE-OUT

A variant of PERFORM-statements which is sometimes useful, is the following:

$$\text{PERFORM procedure-name-1 [THRU procedure-name-2]} \begin{Bmatrix} \text{identifier} \\ \text{integer} \end{Bmatrix} \text{TIMES}$$

With such a statement the indicated procedure is performed as many times as is defined by the number before TIMES, and then a jump is performed back to the statement following the PERFORM-statement. Examples:

PERFORM PERSON-COMP PERSON-NUMBER TIMES
PERFORM WRITE-OUT 10 TIMES
PERFORM P1 THRU P3 T TIMES

There are other options of the verb PERFORM, but their description is deferred to Sections 5.6. and 9.2. since conditions and subscripting must be treated first.

A statement using the verb STOP will cause the computer to halt or the running of the COBOL program to be completed. In the latter case the computer will continue, e.g. compiling the next program. General format:

$$\text{STOP} \begin{Bmatrix} \text{literal} \\ \text{RUN} \end{Bmatrix}$$

45

To indicate that the running of a COBOL program is definitely finished we use the statement STOP RUN. If instead a temporary stop is wanted we ought to choose STOP followed by a literal which will be displayed by the computer when it stops. If the operator then pushes the start button, the computer will continue the program with the statement following directly after the STOP-statement. Examples:

```
STOP   RUN
STOP   2 5
STOP   "WRONG  CARD"
STOP   "CHANGE  TAPE" ;   GO  TO  READ-IN
```

5.6. Conditions

As has been mentioned earlier, one of the most important properties of a computer is that it can choose between different alternatives depending on currently attained results. In COBOL this is described in conditional statements. Previously in Section 5.4. we met such a construction, viz. arithmetic statements containing a SIZE ERROR-element. The subsequent statements in that case will be performed only if the result of the computation has become too large to be stored. Constructions with the verb READ (see 5.7.) are also conditional statements. The effect of a conditional statement depends upon a certain *condition* being fulfilled or not. We shall here discuss two kinds of conditions, viz. relations and class conditions. *Relations* have the format:

$$
\left\{ \begin{array}{l} \text{identifier-1} \\ \text{literal-1} \\ \text{arithmetic-expression-1} \end{array} \right\} \left\{ \begin{array}{l} \text{IS [NOT] GREATER THAN} \\ \text{IS [NOT] LESS THAN} \\ \text{IS [NOT] EQUAL TO} \end{array} \right\} \left\{ \begin{array}{l} \text{identifier-2} \\ \text{literal-2} \\ \text{arithmetic-expression-2} \end{array} \right\}
$$

It is not permissible for both members in a relation to consist of literals. The COBOL words GREATER, LESS, and EQUAL TO entering the format may be replaced by the symbols >, <, and =. The relation is tested by comparing the two members, the result being true if the condition is satisfied, otherwise false. The comparison itself is performed in one way if both members are numeric, in another way if one or both are nonnumeric. If both members are numeric, only their algebraic values are considered, and the numbers 004711, 471100, and 4711 are all EQUAL. At the top of the next page we present a table giving the value of different relations for some numerical values.

If one or both members in a relation are nonnumeric, the comparison is performed character by character. We then have equality if all characters are equal. This is also the case when the two members have different lengths

46

A	B	A > B	A NOT > B	A < B	A NOT < B	A = B	A NOT = B
1	1	false	true	false	true	true	false
1	2	false	true	true	false	false	true
− 1	− 2	true	false	false	true	false	true
− 12	1	false	true	true	false	false	true
810	11	true	false	false	true	false	true

caused by the fact that the longer member has some extra blanks at the end. However, if there are other characters in these positions, the longer item is considered to be GREATER. When the two members have different contents, the magnitude is determined through the so-called *collating sequence* of the computer. For every computer there is a special arrangement defined for all characters allowed in increasing order. These sequences are different for different computers. However, as a rule blank is smallest, then we have digits and letters in the usual order, other characters normally coming at the end of the sequence. As an example we assume that the collating sequence of a certain machine starts with a blank and then is followed by:

0123456789ABCDEFGHIJKLMNOPQRSTUVWXYZ . , + − * / $ ( ) =

The values of some relations are presented in the following table.

A	B	A > B	A < B	A = B
” A D A M ”	” A D A M ”	false	false	true
” A D A M ”	” A D A M ”	false	false	true
” A D A M ”	” E V E ”	false	true	false
” E V E ”	” E V E S ”	false	true	false
” P 1 ”	” P A R ”	false	true	false
” P ”	” P ”	true	false	false
” 3 ”	” T H R E E ”	false	true	false
” P E R . ”	” P E R , ”	false	true	false
” − 6 2 ”	” M I N ”	true	false	false

We give some more examples of relations:

```
TIME  IS  GREATER  THAN  NORM-TIME
X  **  2  +  Y  **  2  LESS  THAN  RADIUS  **  2
SUM-A  NOT  GREATER  THAN  ZERO
PRODUCT-NO  EQUAL  TO  1984
”999”  IS  LESS  ID-OF-GOODS
EVE  IS  NOT  EQUAL  TO  ”EVE”
```

For *class conditions* we have the general format:

$$\text{identifier IS [\underline{NOT}]} \left\{ \begin{array}{l} \underline{\text{NUMERIC}} \\ \underline{\text{ALPHABETIC}} \end{array} \right\}$$

Using this condition we can test if the area reserved for a data item contains digits only or letters and blanks only. Examples:

```
IDENTIFIER IS NUMERIC
IDENTIFIER IS NOT ALPHABETIC
```

In order to indicate explicitly the condition determining the direction of the computations we can use a conditional statement with the verb IF which has the general format:

$$\underline{\text{IF}} \text{ condition} \left\{ \begin{array}{l} \text{statement-1} \\ \underline{\text{NEXT SENTENCE}} \end{array} \right\} \left\{ \begin{array}{l} \underline{\text{ELSE}} \\ \underline{\text{OTHERWISE}} \end{array} \right\} \left\{ \begin{array}{l} \text{statement-2} \\ \underline{\text{NEXT SENTENCE}} \end{array} \right\}$$

The two words ELSE and OTHERWISE are equivalent. Statement-1 denotes one or several statements while statement-2 comprises all statements to the end of the sentence. When an IF-statement is executed the condition is first tested. If it has the value true, the statements before ELSE are performed, otherwise the statements after ELSE. In both cases the following sentence will be executed next (provided no statement performed is a GO-statement). The option NEXT SENTENCE is applied when we want to continue immediately with next sentence. If the words ELSE NEXT SENTENCE come directly before the concluding period, they may be omitted. Examples:

```
IF TIME GREATER THAN NORM-TIME
COMPUTE OVERTIME = TIME - NORM-TIME.
IF SEX EQUAL TO 1 GO TO MAN.
IF SEX EQUAL TO 2 PERFORM WOMAN-CALC
ELSE GO TO WRONG-DATA.
IF BIRTH-NO IS NUMERIC NEXT SENTENCE
ELSE GO TO ERROR-IN-DATA.
IF TIME > NORM-TIME
COMPUTE OVERTIME = TIME - NORM-TIME
ADD 1 TO DILIGENT-PERSONS
COMPUTE EXTRA-SALARY = OVERTIME * HOURLY-PAY
ELSE ADD 1 TO LAZY-PERSONS
MOVE ZERO TO EXTRA-SALARY.
```

In the last example three statements are performed if the condition is true, two if it is false. It might well be the case that some of the statements contained in an IF-statement is again a conditional statement. This gives an easy opportunity to choose between more than two alternatives. Example:

```
I F   T I M E   I S   L E S S   T H A N   7   P E R F O R M   N I G H T - W O R K
E L S E   I F   T I M E   I S   L E S S   T H A N   1 8   P E R F O R M   D A Y - W O R K
E L S E   P E R F O R M   E V E N I N G - W O R K .
```

Here NIGHT – WORK is performed midnight—7 a.m., DAY – WORK 7 a.m.—6 p.m., and EVENING – WORK 6 p.m.—midnight.

When a conditional statement is part of an IF-statement before ELSE, then ELSE plays the same role as a period at the end of a sentence on determining the scope of the conditional statement. Examples:

```
I F   I N D   =   1   A D D   1 0 0   T O   T I M E   O N   S I Z E   E R R O R
M O V E   0   T O   I N D   M O V E   1   T O   B   E L S E   S U B T R A C T   D   F R O M   A .

I F   K   <   1 5 0   A D D   1   T O   K   I F   T   A L P H A B E T I C   M O V E   T
T O   A B T   G O   T O   P 1   E L S E   M O V E   T   T O   A N T   G O   T O   P 2
E L S E   N E X T   S E N T E N C E .
```

In the first example the statements MOVE 0 TO IND and MOVE 1 TO B are performed only if the result of the addition becomes too large to be stored. In the last example, if K is less than 150 and T is not alphabetic, the statement ADD 1 TO K and the statements between the first and the second ELSE are executed.

It sometimes happens that the execution of a computation is dependent on several conditions. This situation can be described by a series of IF-statements after each other and jumps between them with GO- statements. However, a solution along these lines becomes rather clumsy, and in fact COBOL offers a possibility of combining several conditions into one condition by use of logical operators. There are three logical operators, viz. OR, AND, and NOT. Their actions are explained through the following table where A and B are conditions which can assume the values true or false.

| A | true | true | false | false |
B	true	false	true	false
A OR B	true	true	true	false
A AND B	true	false	false	false
NOT A	false	false	true	true

We can combine several conditional expressions in a way similar to the construction of arithmetic expressions. Parentheses around an expression will imply that its value is evaluated first as is the case with an arithmetic expression. When no parentheses are present the evaluation takes place in the following order:

1. arithmetic operators   4. AND
2. relational operators   5. OR
3. NOT

In a few examples we shall try to illustrate the structure of compound conditional expressions. Suppose that we want to terminate a certain

computation if PERSON – NUMBER is greater than TOTAL – NUMBER or if
VOLUNTARIES has reached the value NEED – OF – PEOPLE or if both these
conditions are valid simultaneously. It is obvious that OR is the correct
logical operator. Thus we obtain:

```
IF  PERSON-NUMBER  IS  GREATER  THAN  TOTAL-NUMBER
OR  VOLUNTARIES  IS  EQUAL  TO  NEED-OF-PEOPLE
GO  TO  COMPLETION.
```

In our second example we consider the conditional expression

```
A + B  GREATER  C  AND  16  LESS  R  OR  NOT  C  -  X  LESS  2
```

and evaluate it when A = 2, B = 3, C = 6, X = 4, and R = 19.48. Observing
the order for the different operations we find that the value is true according to the following scheme:

```
A + B  GREATER  C  AND  16  LESS  R  OR  NOT  C  -  X  LESS  2
   5                                            2
─────────┘└──────────┘  └───────┘└───────┘  ────────┘└──────────┘
   false        true          false
─────────────┘└──────────────┘  └───────────────┘└──────────────┘
     false                            true
─────────────────────────┘└──────────────────────────┘
              true
```

When we are using the verb PERFORM (cf. 5.5.) we can let the number
of executions of a certain piece of program be determined by a condition.
Such a statement has the format:

PERFORM procedure-name-1 [THRU procedure-name-2]
    UNTIL condition-1

This statement causes condition-1 to be tested and if its value is false the
indicated procedure is performed; then condition-1 is tested anew and if its
value still turns out false the procedure is performed again. As soon as the
value of the condition becomes true a return jump to the statement after
the PERFORM-statement is accomplished. If the condition happens to be
true when the PERFORM-statement is encountered, the procedure is not at
all executed. The condition can contain e.g. a variable which is changed
each time the procedure is traversed. Examples:

```
PERFORM  READ-IN  UNTIL  PERSONS  IS  EQUAL  TO
PERSONS-TOTAL
PERFORM  PAYMENT  UNTIL  DEBT  IS  NOT  GREATER  ZERO
```

It often happens that the number of repetitions is determined by a tally,
i.e. a variable whose value is increased by a constant amount each time the
indicated part of the program is performed. In this case we can use a
PERFORM-statement with the format:

PERFORM procedure-name-1 [THRU procedure-name-2]
  VARYING identifier-1

  FROM $\left\{ \begin{array}{l} \text{literal-2} \\ \text{identifier-2} \end{array} \right\}$ BY $\left\{ \begin{array}{l} \text{literal-3} \\ \text{identifier-3} \end{array} \right\}$ UNTIL condition-1

When such a statement is executed, identifier-1 is first set equal to
identifier-2 (literal-2). Then condition-1 is tested, and if it has the value
false, the indicated procedure is traversed. After that identifier-3 (literal-3)
is added to identifier-1 and condition-1 tested again to determine if
another repetition will take place. If on the other hand the condition has
the value true, then control passes directly to the next statement. Example:

PERFORM READ-IN VARYING PERSONS FROM 1 BY 1
UNTIL PERSONS IS GREATER THAN PERSONS-TOTAL

We are now going to define more carefully the rules which must be
applied to PERFORM-statements. In the statement PERFORM P1 THRU P2
it is not necessary that P1 and P2 are both paragraph-names or both section-
names; a mixture is also allowed. It should be observed that the last
sentence in the procedure controlled by a PERFORM-statement must not
contain a GO-statement. Otherwise one or more GO-statements are per-
fectly legitimate, provided that we always, sooner or later, arrive at the
last sentence of P2 (or P1 if THRU P2 is missing). In order to facilitate the
choice of different computation paths within the procedure, it is sometimes
found convenient to let P2 consist of just one statement, viz. the verb
EXIT. This word plays the role of a dummy statement where the different
paths join together and from which the jump back is performed. It is permissible for the procedure controlled by a PERFORM-statement in turn to
contain other PERFORM-statements. However, in such cases the corresponding procedures must lie either completely inside or completely outside
the procedure, P1 through P2, controlled by the first PERFORM-statement.
By use of some schematic figures we shall try to illustrate how the nesting of
different PERFORM-statements may be carried out.

P0.   PERFORM P1 THRU P7.

P1.
P2.   PERFORM P4 THRU P6.   Allowed nesting. The procedure con-
P3.   trolled by the statement in P2 lies com-
P4.   pletely inside the procedure controlled
P5.   by the statement in P0.
P6.
P7.

P0.

P1.

P2. PERFORM P3 THRU P4.

P3. PERFORM P0 THRU P1.

P4.

Allowed nesting. The procedures controlled by the statement in P2 and the statement in P3 are completely disjoint.

P0. PERFORM P1 THRU P2.

P1. PERFORM P2 THRU P4.

P2.

P3.

P4.

Forbidden nesting. The procedure controlled by the statement in P1 partly overlaps the procedure controlled by the statement in P0.

The dynamic definition of a procedure has the effect that also constructions of the following kind are allowed:

```
P0. PERFORM P1 THRU P2.
    . . .
P2. . . .
    . . .
P1. . . .
    GO TO P2.
```

An example of a part of a procedure division containing several PERFORM-statements is as follows. We assume that we have a set of persons. The record PERSON is supposed to contain information on, among other things, SEX (1 for men, 2 for women) and CHILDREN (number of children). In the procedure division there is one paragraph, CHILDREN – SUBSIDY performing write-out of a subsidy-check for a woman with children. There is also a paragraph MAINTENANCE – GRANT which controls for men with children if they have to pay maintenance; if this is the case an invoice on the amount should be produced.

```
MAIN-PROGRAM.
     PERFORM PERSON-COMPUTATION THRU PERSON-READY
     VARYING PERSON-NUMBER FROM 1 BY 1 UNTIL
     PERSON-NUMBER IS GREATER THAN PERSON-TOTAL.
     GO TO READY.
PERSON-COMPUTATION.  . . .
     GO TO MAN WOMAN DEPENDING ON SEX.
MAN. PERFORM MAINTENANCE-GRANT CHILDREN TIMES.
     GO TO PERSON-READY.
WOMAN. PERFORM CHILDREN-SUBSIDY CHILDREN TIMES.
PERSON-READY. EXIT.
MAINTENANCE-GRANT.  . . .
CHILDREN-SUBSIDY.  . . .
READY.  . . .
```

5.7. Input-output

Input-output may be defined as all operations transferring data to and from the internal storage of the computer. Well-known examples are read-in of data from punched cards or punched tape or storing data on magnetic tapes or disks. The data to be transferred are usually organized as *files*, consisting of records normally in a sequential order.

On input operations for files, records are transferred from an external unit to the internal storage; for output operations the transfers go in the opposite direction. The records in a file may be accessible only sequentially which means that they must be treated in a predetermined order. If, for example, we have data represented on punched cards, every item occupying certain columns, then each card may correspond to one record and the whole deck constitute a file. On an input operation the card is read and its information placed in a suitable space in the internal storage. When the information has been processed the next card is read, and so on. In a like manner records placed on magnetic tapes are processed in a sequence, one after the other.

In conjunction with all input-output operations checking of several different kinds is automatically performed by the computer. For example, an automatic check determines whether there are data available for read-in operations, and whether there is free storage space when an output operation is initiated. There are also other checks to make sure the transfers are accurate.

There are six verbs in COBOL designed for input-output, viz. ACCEPT and DISPLAY for small amounts of data, and OPEN, READ, WRITE, and CLOSE which are used for the bulk of the work in reading and writing files. The verbs READ and WRITE are used for transfers of records between external units and the internal storage, while OPEN and CLOSE initiate and finish required controls on transfers of files.

When we want to use a file for reading or writing, the file must first be opened which is done by a statement containing the verb OPEN. This does not give rise to a transfer of data records to or from the internal storage but only serves to prepare the necessary hardware units for reading or writing. For a file on magnetic tape this can imply a rewind of the tape so that the reading-head comes at the beginning of the tape. On files stored on magnetic tapes or disks there may be special label records, before the records proper, containing information as to the name of the file and other identification data. When a file is opened for writing, the very first record is a label which is written according to specifications given in the data division of the program. When the same file is opened later for reading the previously written label may be checked to make sure it is the correct file being read. A statement with the verb OPEN has the format:

$$\text{OPEN} \left\{ \begin{array}{ll} \underline{\text{INPUT}} & \{\text{file-name-1}\} \dots [\underline{\text{OUTPUT}} \ \{\text{file-name-2}\} \dots] \\ \underline{\text{OUTPUT}} & \{\text{file-name-1}\} \dots [\underline{\text{INPUT}} \quad \{\text{file-name-2}\} \dots] \end{array} \right\}$$

Here INPUT is used when data are to be read from a file, OUTPUT when data are to be written on a file. Examples:

```
OPEN  INPUT  NEW-PERSONS
OPEN  INPUT  INFILE  OUTPUT  WRITEFILE,  ERRORFILE
```

The verb READ has the effect that the next data record is transferred from a file in an external unit to the internal storage. The data items which belong to the record are then available for processing in the procedure division under the names they were given in a record description in the data division. A READ-statement has the following format:

<u>READ</u> file-name RECORD [<u>INTO</u> identifier]; AT <u>END</u> imperative-statement

After reading, the information of the record is available in the record area reserved for the file. It should be observed that only the information of the current record is accessible. However, by using the INTO option it is possible to move it to a working storage or to the area of a record belonging to an output file. The imperative statement after END in the format above is executed when there are no more records in the file because all have been read earlier. Such an attempt to read a record from a file which does not contain more records must not be made more than once. Examples:

```
READ  PERSON-IN  AT  END  PERFORM  TERMINATION
STOP  RUN.
READ  INFILE  RECORD  INTO  SECONDARY  AT  END  GO  TO
WRITE-OUT.
```

When a data record is to be transferred from the internal storage to a file on an external unit the verb WRITE is used. For files stored on magnetic tape there is an automatic check to determine if there is space available on the tape; otherwise suitable steps are taken, e.g. rewind, stop for change of tapes, or switching to another tape unit. A statement with the verb WRITE has the format:

<u>WRITE</u> record-name [<u>FROM</u> identifier-1]

$$\left[\left\{ \begin{array}{l} \underline{\text{BEFORE}} \\ \underline{\text{AFTER}} \end{array} \right\} \text{ADVANCING} \left\{ \begin{array}{l} \text{identifier-2 LINES} \\ \text{integer LINES} \\ \text{mnemonic-name} \end{array} \right\} \right]$$

Note that we here use the record-name as distinguished from OPEN, READ, and CLOSE where the file-name is used. After the writing, the information of the record is no longer available. If the FROM option is used the information in identifier-1 is first moved to the record, and after that the writing is accomplished. As is the case when a MOVE-statement is executed, the contents of identifier-1 are then left unchanged.

When a printer is used for output, each record as a rule occupies one line, and line shift is performed automatically, either before or after the writing, depending on the hardware. The ADVANCING option gives the programmer means to control the line shift directly. The mnemonic name must then be defined in the environment division of the program and usually defines certain fixed positions on a page by the aid of holes in a control tape in the line printer. The effect of an ADVANCING option is obvious: if AFTER is used, the writing is performed after the line shift, with BEFORE the writing occurs before the line shift. Examples:

```
WRITE  PERSON-OUT
WRITE  INCOME-TAX AFTER ADVANCING 3 LINES
WRITE  EXEMPTION FROM TAX-EXEMPT
WRITE  TOTAL-TAX BEFORE ADVANCING NEW-PAGE
```

We have mentioned earlier that before the records in a file can be read and written with the verbs READ and WRITE, it is necessary to open the file by the aid of an OPEN-statement. When all records in a file have been processed, the file must be closed which is accomplished by the verb CLOSE. The effect of a CLOSE-statement varies depending on the nature of the file. For example, an output file on magnetic tape may be provided with an ending label; with an input file it may be checked by controlling the ending label that all records have been read correctly. If the file is stored on magnetic tape a rewind operation is also initiated through the verb CLOSE. It has the format:

CLOSE file-name-1 [, file-name-2] ...

Examples:

```
CLOSE  FILE-2
CLOSE  A-FILE,  B-FILE,  C-FILE
CLOSE  INFILE OUTFILE
```

When we want to read or write data which cannot conveniently be arranged in files, we can use the verbs ACCEPT and DISPLAY. We are here almost always concerned with small amounts of data to be fed in or out on some isolated occasions when the program is run on the computer. Then it is not necessary to consider entire records; also groups or elementary items can occur.

ACCEPT causes input of a data item from an external unit to the internal storage. It has the general format:

ACCEPT identifier [FROM mnemonic-name]

Here identifier denotes a group or a single elementary item. Very often there is a standard unit for input with the verb ACCEPT, e.g. an on-line type writer. In other cases the mnemonic name, which is defined in the environment division, shows which unit should be used. Examples of ACCEPT-statements:

```
ACCEPT DATE
ACCEPT TOTAL-NUMBER FROM CARDS
ACCEPT BOUNDS FROM TAPE-IN
```

The verb DISPLAY is used for output of small amounts of data, usually occasional information to the operator, e.g. concerning errors in the data or termination of the run. As is the case with the verb ACCEPT there is often a special unit assigned to these communications, e.g. a console type-writer or a display screen. The verb DISPLAY has the following general format:

$$\text{DISPLAY} \left\{ \begin{array}{l} \text{literal-1} \\ \text{identifier-1} \end{array} \right\} \left[\begin{array}{l} \text{, literal-2} \\ \text{, identifier-2} \end{array} \right] \dots [\text{UPON} \ \text{mnemonic-name}]$$

Examples:

```
DISPLAY DATE UPON SHEET
DISPLAY "DATE OF THE DAY " DATE
DISPLAY MONTH "/" DAY "/" YEAR
```

If we suppose that DATE consists of three elementary items, MONTH, DAY, and YEAR with 2, 2, and 4 decimal digits, we would obtain the following print-outs with the three DISPLAY-statements on the 13th of February, 1984:

```
02131984
DATE OF THE DAY 02131984
02/13/1984
```

Further examples:

```
DISPLAY "ADAM"
DISPLAY QUOTE "ADAM" QUOTE
DISPLAY "ADAM" QUOTE "S"
```

Executing these DISPLAY-statements we obtain the following print-outs: ADAM, "ADAM", and ADAM"S.

5.8. Example

In order to illustrate the complete structure of the procedure division of a COBOL program we shall give an example as a conclusion to this chapter. We assume that on magnetic tape we have a file, DEBTFILE, containing a type of records DEBT – INSTALMENT which consists of the two elementary items INITIAL – DEBT and INSTALMENT. Every debt, initially amounting to INITIAL – DEBT dollars, is to be repaid with fixed yearly instalments, i.e. at the end of every YEAR the amount INSTALMENT has to be paid (except, of course, the last year when the amount is generally less). The instalment consists of AMORTIZATION and INTEREST. For each initial debt an amortization plan should be constructed, and for each YEAR the five elementary items YEAR, INDEBT, AMORTIZATION, INTEREST, and OUTDEBT, together forming a record PAYMENT in the output file AMORTIZATION – PLAN, should be written out. Two auxiliary variables T and OUTDEBT – TEMP are used to keep the values of YEAR and OUTDEBT which are lost each time the record PAYMENT is written. The rate of interest in per cent is the same for all debts and is read at the beginning of the program by an ACCEPT-statement.

```
PROCEDURE DIVISION.
P1. ACCEPT RATE.
     OPEN INPUT DEBTFILE OUTPUT AMORTIZATION-PLAN.
READ-IN. READ DEBTFILE AT END
     CLOSE DEBTFILE AMORTIZATION-PLAN STOP RUN.
     MOVE INITIAL-DEBT TO INDEBT.
     PERFORM YEARLY-PAYMENT VARYING T FROM 1 BY 1
     UNTIL INDEBT IS NOT GREATER THAN ZERO.
     GO TO READ-IN.
YEARLY-PAYMENT.
     MOVE T TO YEAR.
     COMPUTE INTEREST = INDEBT * RATE / 100.
     COMPUTE OUTDEBT OUTDEBT-TEMP =
     INDEBT + INTEREST - INSTALMENT.
     IF OUTDEBT IS LESS THAN ZERO MOVE ZERO TO
     OUTDEBT.
     SUBTRACT OUTDEBT FROM INDEBT GIVING
     AMORTIZATION.
     WRITE PAYMENT.
     MOVE OUTDEBT-TEMP TO INDEBT.
```

The procedure division starts with the heading PROCEDURE DIVISION and contains three paragraphs P1, READ – IN, and YEARLY – PAYMENT. In the first paragraph the rate of interest is accepted from the standard input unit and the files are opened for reading and writing. In the paragraph READ – IN the records of DEBTFILE are read one by one. When all the records have been treated the files are closed and the execution of the program is terminated by a STOP RUN-statement. When one record has been read INITIAL – DEBT is transferred to INDEBT and the paragraph YEARLY – PAYMENT, which computes and writes out the payment for one year in the amortization plan, is performed until the initial debt has been paid. For every execution of YEARLY – PAYMENT the variable T indicating the year is increased by 1. After the completion of the PERFORM-statement the program is ready to treat the next record of DEBTFILE. In the paragraph YEARLY – PAYMENT the values of the five elementary items of the record PAYMENT are computed and then this record is written out. If the computed value of OUTDEBT happens to be negative, this indicates that the remaining debt is less than the instalment and the value zero is transferred to OUTDEBT. The auxiliary variable OUTDEBT – TEMP is used to initialize INDEBT of the next year.

Exercises

1. Assume that A = 1, B = 5, C = 3, D = 10, and E = − 7 before each of the statements below is executed. Find the values of the identifiers after the execution of the statements.

    a) MOVE A TO B
    b) MOVE A TO D E
    c) MOVE 1 5 TO A
    d) ADD A B C
    e) ADD B TO C
    f) ADD A TO D E
    g) ADD B C D TO A
    h) ADD D E GIVING B
    i) SUBTRACT B FROM D
    j) SUBTRACT B FROM D GIVING D E
    k) SUBTRACT C D E FROM A
    l) MULTIPLY B BY C
    m) MULTIPLY C BY A B C
    n) MULTIPLY C BY D GIVING E
    o) DIVIDE B INTO D GIVING E
    p) DIVIDE − 5 INTO B D
    q) DIVIDE B BY 2 GIVING E
    r) COMPUTE C = (D + E) ∗∗ 2 − A
    s) COMPUTE A D = A ∗ B + C ∗ E

2. Write statements which compute the following expressions, first by use of ADD, SUBTRACT, MULTIPLY, and DIVIDE, and then by use of the verb COMPUTE. In the former case an identifier H may be applied for intermediary results.

a) $\quad$ S $\;=\;$ S $\;+\;$ T

b) $\quad$ S $\;=\;$ S $\;+\;$ T^2

c) $\quad$ B $\;=\;$ P $\;\cdot\;$ K $\;+\;$ A

d) $\quad$ ITEM-PRIZE $\;=\;$ PURCHASE-PRIZE $\;+\;$ COST $\;/\;$ QUANT

3. Write a conditional statement assigning the values -1, 0, or $+1$ to SIGNUM depending on $X<0$, $X=0$, or $X>0$.

4. Construct a statement with the effect that a jump is performed to the paragraph ERROR – IN – DATA if CODEX contains other than alphabetic characters.

5. The sum $1+\dfrac{1}{2}+\dfrac{1}{3}+\dfrac{1}{4}+\dfrac{1}{5}+\ldots$ can grow beyond any limit if a sufficient number of terms is taken. Write a paragraph SUMMATION which increases the value of the sum by an arbitrary term $1/K$. Then use this paragraph-name in a PERFORM-statement entering a computation for deciding how many terms are necessary for making the sum greater than 10. The number of terms should be written out by a DISPLAY-statement.

6. Assume that we have a file EXPERIMENT – FILE with records containing among other things an elementary item OBS – X representing a measured physical quantity. Construct the procedure division of a COBOL program which computes the number of records where OBS – X is greater than 0 and less than 10. The sum and the sum of the squares of these OBS – X should also be computed. The three results should be written out by a DISPLAY-statement.

Chapter 6. The data division

I never read, I just look at pictures.

ANDY WARHOL

6.1. Introduction

arious operations such as reading, writing, and arithmetic operations which may be performed on data were described in the preceding chapter on the procedure division. The specification of such operations is only part of the solution of a data processing problem. The programmer must also specify the characteristics of the files and data items so that necessary transfers and computations may be carried out. The purpose of the *data division* in a COBOL program is to give the detailed specifications for all the files and data items which are required in the program.

The data division and the procedure division are very closely connected. The data division has a decisive influence on the way in which the verbs in the procedure division actually complete their actions. For example, consider the statement

MOVE A TO B.

This statement implies a lot more than a simple move of the contents of the area reserved for A into the corresponding area for B. If the information in A and B is represented in different ways, the contents of A must be converted to the form given for B. If A is numeric the transfer may also imply editing, e.g. so that leading zeros in A are replaced by blanks or asterisks. Which operations are actually performed at a transfer depends on how the data items concerned are described in the data division. The data descriptions thus determine the exact form of the part of the object program which handles the transfer.

By separating the description of data from the processing of data one can attain several advantages. The source program becomes more perspicuous, and the separation forces a logical and hence effective fashion of tackling the problem. Further the separation of description from processing offers a flexible way to make changes in the program. Some problems in administrative data processing are of such a character that the corresponding programs may be run over and over many times without any changes whatsoever required. More likely, however, is that the program will have to be periodically modified and updated as conditions change. For example, changes in salary regulations have certain obvious effects on a program for computing salaries. The changes can influence not only the form of the data but also the computation itself. In the former case we have to modify the data division, in the latter case the procedure division. While even apparently small changes, e.g. an increase of the internal storage area for a certain data item, may necessitate a time-consuming reprogramming for a machine-coded program, the corresponding change for a COBOL program will only claim a small modification in the data division and a recompilation. In this way a new object program is quickly produced and can be used for processing along the new lines.

With respect to how data are treated during processing they can be divided into three groups, viz. data organized in *files* for transfer to or from the internal storage of the computer, *intermediary results* created in the memory and stored in a working-storage, and *constants* which are specific for a given problem and defined by the programmer. Starting from these categories we divide the data division into three sections, the file section, the working-storage section, and the constant section.

The sections consist of a series of *entries*, each describing one unit of data. An entry can be independent or related to other entries. The connection is expressed by a level indicator or a level number in the beginning of the entry. Then comes the name of the data unit generally followed by a number of *clauses* defining special properties of the data unit. Refraining from details we here give a few examples where the file ARTICLES with level indicator FD and the data item PERSON – NO with level number 03 are specified.

```
FD    ARTICLES;  LABEL  RECORDS  ARE  OMITTED;
      DATA  RECORD  IS  COM.
03    PERSON-NO;  PICTURE  IS  9999.
```

The *file section* contains a description of the files. A file is a sequence of records which are fetched from or transferred to an external unit, e.g. a magnetic tape unit, a card reader, or a card punch. The individual records on the file can have different structures and sizes, each type requiring its own special description. The physical properties of a file must be distinguished from its logical properties. Examples of physical properties are the recording mode, how the records are grouped together into blocks on the external unit, and information about the identification of the file. Logical properties are the characteristics of the records and their subordinate data items in the file. The description of a file starts with a file description entry.

Here a name is assigned to the file and the physical properties described. After that there are one or more entries describing the records contained in the file.

Data which have no connection with the external units but instead are stored in the internal storage of the computer are described in the *working-storage section*. In the area defined in this way one can store for example intermediary results in numerical computations, data for administration of the program, and intermediary information concerning transfers from one file to another.

It is possible to group data items into records not only in the file section but also in the working-storage and constant sections. Moreover, in these two sections there are also elementary items with a special type of level numbers indicating that such an item is completely independent with regard to other data items. Further, in the working-storage section initial values may be assigned to the data items which are to be starting values of the data items when execution of the procedure division begins. In the *constant section* the programmer may assign names to his constants. In this way the procedure division becomes more readable and changes of the value of a constant is facilitated because we only have to change the value of the constant in one place in the data division instead of in several places in the procedure division. The constant section is organized in almost the same way as the working-storage section. The essential difference is that we are not allowed to change the contents in a storage area reserved through the constant section by a statement in the procedure division.

Finally we give some rules concerning the form of the data division in the COBOL program. After the header

DATA DIVISION.

we have in order the three sections, each beginning with the name and the word SECTION with a period:

FILE SECTION.
WORKING – STORAGE SECTION.
CONSTANT SECTION.

In the same line as a section header no other text may occur. If a section is not needed for the definition of a certain problem, the section can be left out completely.

6.2. Description of records and data items

The record description aims at giving a detailed account of the properties of the data items in the COBOL program. For each data item we write an entry consisting of a level number, a data-name, and in general one or more clauses. The level numbers are used to show how the record is organized in groups. The data-name is used as a reference to the data item. The clauses are used to assign a variety of possible properties to the data item, such as size, category, and usage. If the data item is a numeric elementary item, then the position of the decimal point as well as a possible occurrence of plus and minus signs can be specified in a clause. Further, rules for the editing of data can be given, and it is also possible to indicate how many times an element is repeated in a table or a list. An entry can appear in many different forms. As a rule, we make a complete description only of elementary items since the properties of a group depends on the properties of the subordinate elementary items.

The information in a record usually consists of particulars describing a certain individual. For example, a record in a file of employees in a company may contain information about name, department, salary per hour, tax conditions, and so on. If we want to refer to and process this information we must subdivide the record into smaller units. This subdivision process can then be repeated to make more detailed references possible. In this way we get different *levels* of subdivisions of a record. A data item which occurs in a later subdivision belongs to a lower level than one which has been obtained earlier. As an example we consider a record TIME – CARD which has been subdivided into four main groups, three of them containing subgroups:

The data items which cannot be subdivided further constitute the elementary items of the record and can appear on all levels. For example, the elementary item HOURS belongs to a higher level than the elementary item MONTH. Often one wants to refer to a whole group of elementary items, especially when data are moved. In COBOL this is done by using the comprehensive data-name for these. In the example we can thus treat the elementary items MONTH, DAY, and YEAR simultaneously by referring to the data item DATE. Referring to TIME – CARD we can reach all eight elementary items of the record. The described way of subdividing records implies that only adjacent elementary items in the record can be brought together to form a group. The elementary items MONTH and YEAR cannot form a group since the item DAY comes in between.

In COBOL *level numbers* are used to indicate how the elementary items in a record are organized. The level number is a two-digit integer placed at the beginning of the entry of each group and elementary item. The record which is the most extensive group is given the level number 01 while other data items are given larger level numbers not to exceed 49. In the level numbers 01 through 09 zero may be replaced by a blank. The level numbers 66, 77, and 88 have special tasks and will be discussed later. In general, subordinate data items have higher level numbers than the nearest superior group. We demonstrate the technique with level numbers on the previous example.

```
0 1    TIME-CARD
       0 3  NAME
              0 4   SURNAME
              0 4   FIRST-NAME
       0 3  EMPLOYMENT-NUMBER
              0 4   DEPT
              0 4   DEPT-NO
       0 3  DATE
              1 2  MONTH
              1 2  DAY
              1 2  YEAR
       0 3  HOURS
```

A group comprises all subsequent groups and elementary items until a data item is found with lower or equal level number. In the example the group NAME contains the elementary items SURNAME and FIRST–NAME. The elementary item HOURS does not belong to the group DATE since it has the same level number as DATE.

From the example it is also evident that the level numbers need not come in the natural order 01, 02, 03, 04, ...; for the elementary item DAY we have the order 01, 03, 12. However, all data items belonging to the same nearest superior group must have the same level number. For this reason the following example is not correct:

```
0 1    ABLE
       0 3  BAKER
              0 5   CHARLIE
              0 5   DOG
       0 2  EASY
```

Since BAKER has the level number 03, EASY cannot have the level number 02. Possible numbers are 01, 03, 05, and numbers greater than 05. In the case 01, EASY is an independent record and in the case 03 an elementary item subordinate to the record ABLE and on the same level as the group BAKER. In the case 05, EASY is subordinate to the group BAKER and on the same level as CHARLIE and DOG. Finally, if the level number is greater than 05, EASY will be subordinate to the group DOG. Note that DOG in the last case is a group with only one element, viz. EASY. DOG and EASY can then be interpreted as alternative names for the same elementary item.

Through the arrangement with level numbers we define a certain grouping of data, and it is then left to the computer to create an object program working in agreement with this. We can presume that the program will automatically take the level structure of a data item into account when a reference is made to it from the procedure division. For example, if we write

MOVE DATE TO DATE-1

where DATE is defined as in the example, the statement will have the effect that the contents of the elementary items MONTH, DAY, and YEAR will be transferred to the memory area reserved for DATE-1.

When names are assigned in the data division to the data items, it is suitable to use different names in order to facilitate references. However, for data items belonging to different hierarchies of subdivisions the same data-name may be used. In order to avoid confusion when a reference is made with a data-name used in different meanings, we must combine it with a data-name on a higher level to eliminate all risks for misinterpretation. Such a data-name is called a *qualifier* and does not necessarily have to belong to the level closest above. Formally, a *qualified data-name* is formed by writing the *connective* IN between the original data-name and the qualifier. If this is not enough to secure uniqueness, we can write another IN followed by a qualifier on a still higher level. Since the file-name in each hierarchy belongs to the highest level, it is obvious that file-names must be unique. Examples of qualified data-names:

DEPT IN TIME-CARD

DAY IN DATE IN TIME-CARD

These two examples refer to the record TIME-CARD which has been discussed previously in this section. Instead of the connective IN we can use the word OF which is completely equivalent. Now consider the following two records:

```
1   REG-RECORD                1   NEW-REG-RECORD
    2   INSURANCE-NO               2   INSURANCE-NO
    2   NAME                       2   NAME
    2   BIRTH-DATE                 2   BIRTH-DATE
        3   YEAR                       3   YEAR
        3   MONTH                      3   MONTH
        3   DAY                        3   DAY
    2   DUE                        2   DUE
        3   MONTH                      3   MONTH
        3   DAY                        3   DAY
```

We can refer to the elementary item MONTH in the group BIRTH – DATE of the first record by using the qualified data-name MONTH OF BIRTH – DATE OF REG – RECORD. In a similar way the data-name DAY OF DUE OF NEW – REG – RECORD is applied. It should be mentioned that it is permissible to use a qualified data-name even if it is not required to guarantee uniqueness. It is also permissible to use more qualifiers than necessary. If there are several combinations of qualifiers by which a data item can be defined uniquely, then any one of them may be used. In the example above we can refer to YEAR in BIRTH – DATE in REG – RECORD by YEAR OF BIRTH – DATE OF REG – RECORD or just by YEAR OF REG – RECORD.

We have mentioned earlier that a data description entry consists of a level number, a data-name, and as a rule one or more clauses. There are several different kinds of clauses, and we shall here treat the most important ones. Their formats can be seen from the following entry skeleton.

level-number data-name-1

[; PICTURE IS character-string]

$\left[; \text{USAGE IS} \left\{ \begin{array}{l} \text{COMPUTATIONAL} \\ \text{DISPLAY} \end{array} \right\} \right]$

$\left[; \text{OCCURS} \left\{ \begin{array}{l} \text{integer-1 TIMES} \\ \text{integer-2 TO integer-3 TIMES [DEPENDING ON data-name-2]} \end{array} \right\} \right]$

$\left[; \text{SYNCHRONIZED} \left\{ \begin{array}{l} \text{LEFT} \\ \text{RIGHT} \end{array} \right\} \right]$

[; JUSTIFIED RIGHT]

[; VALUE IS literal].

All clauses in the format are optional and the choice of clauses is determined by the properties which the corresponding data item ought to possess. Unless we are using special devices described in Chapter 9 the PICTURE-clause is compulsory if the data item is an elementary item. The clauses may be written in arbitrary order, but the last clause of a data description entry must be followed by a period. If no clauses are present the period is placed directly after the data-name.

When writing data descriptions in a COBOL program one must be careful to obey the rules for the reference format (cf. 4.8.). Every entry must start on a new line. The level number of a record starts at the A-margin and its record-name at the B-margin. Other entries can start either at the A-margin or at different places to the right in order to make the level structure of the record clear. If the latter way is chosen the entry of a subordinate data item must begin four positions to the right of the preceding one. We illustrate the two possibilities by an example where clauses have been indicated by dots.

66

```
0 1   ARTICLE  ...              0 1   ARTICLE  ...
0 2   ITEM-NO  ...              0 2   ITEM-NO  ...
0 2   QUANTITY  ...             0 2   QUANTITY  ...
0 2   CUSTOMER  ...             0 2   CUSTOMER  ...
0 3   CUSTOMER-NO  ...               0 3   CUSTOMER-NO  ...
0 4   NR  ...                        0 4   NR  ...
0 4   CATEGORY  ...                  0 4   CATEGORY  ...
0 3   DISTRICT  ...                  0 3   DISTRICT  ...
0 2   DELIVERY  ...             0 2   DELIVERY  ...
0 2   PRICE  ...                0 2   PRICE  ...
0 2   SALESMAN  ...             0 2   SALESMAN  ...
```

When the second way of writing is chosen it is not necessary to use indentation for every new level number as is shown for the items NR and CATEGORY of CUSTOMER – NO. If an entry needs more space than one line, the following lines must not begin to the left of the B-margin or the preceding line.

6.3. The picture of the elementary item

There are three different categories of elementary items in COBOL. Numeric elementary items are allowed to contain only the digits 0, 1, 2, ... 9 together with an indication of the sign of the number. Alphabetic elementary items can only contain letters and blanks, while alphanumeric elementary items can contain arbitrary characters. The *size* of a data item is defined as the number of characters contained in the item. When a data item is a group the size is the total number of characters in all the subordinate elementary items.

We shall now consider the clause

PICTURE IS character-string

which is only used in descriptions of elementary items. The character string in the format is called the *picture* of the elementary item and consists of certain allowed combinations of COBOL characters. The picture must not contain more than 30 characters, and primarily it describes the general properties of an elementary item such as size, category, number of decimals, all of them influencing the memory space reserved on compilation and the interpretation of the contents when the object program is executed. Further the picture is used to specify editing for printing purposes.

There are 17 different symbols which can enter the character string after PICTURE. Out of the 17 symbols 6 are general and 11 are used for editing purposes. The meaning of the 6 general symbols along with the nature of the corresponding data item are shown in the table at the top of the next page. The symbols 9, S, V, and P are used to describe *numeric* elementary items where no editing is to be performed when data are moved to the storage area reserved for the item.

Symbol		Meaning
9	Numeric	Digit
S	Numeric	Operational sign
V	Numeric	Assumed decimal point
P	Numeric	Assumed decimal position
A	Alphabetic	Letter or blank
X	Alphanumeric	COBOL character

Every digit 9 in the picture represents a character position containing one decimal digit. If we want to describe the elementary item A as a five-digit positive integer we can write

04   A PICTURE IS 99999.

Alternatively we can write

04   A PICTURE IS 9(5).

The digit 5 within parentheses indicates that the symbol 9 occurs five times in sequence. This mode of description can be applied to all symbols which can appear more than once in a picture; for example *(7) is equivalent to *******.

The letter S is used to indicate that an elementary item has a plus or minus sign. The S must come first in the picture. Such an elementary item can assume both positive and negative values when present in arithmetic operations and relation tests or when it receives numerical data in a MOVE-statement. This type of sign is called *operational* and should not be confused with the alphanumeric symbols + and − which are used to show that a printed number is positive or negative. The operational sign is not included in the size of the elementary item and from the programmer's viewpoint it may be assumed that the sign can be stored in the computer without occupying a character position of its own. (Often some free bit-position, e.g. in the space for a digit, can be used internally to store the sign.) If we write the statement MOVE −7 TO B where B is described through

03   B PICTURE IS S999.

then B will afterwards contain $00\overline{7}$. In the sequel we represent the operational sign by + or − placed above the last digit in the number, in this way indicating that the sign does not use a special character position. In this case the size of B is 3 positions.

The letter V is used to indicate the position of an assumed decimal point and hence cannot appear more than once in a picture. As is the case for S, the letter V does not represent a special character position and is not counted when the size of the elementary item is determined. In the examples

```
0 5    A  PICTURE  IS  999V99.
0 5    B  PICTURE  99V999.
```

the data-name A represents a number with 3 integer digits and 2 decimals while B represents a number with 2 integer digits and 3 decimals. It should be observed that no decimal point is present in the elementary item as a character. The purpose of the assumed decimal point is to define a scale factor to be applied to the contents of the storage area when the numerical value is treated in the program. Thus, if A contains 52394, it represents the value 523.94 while the same contents in B would mean 52.394. Hence, the areas for A and B are treated differently by the object program. In numerical computations and on transfers data are automatically aligned according to the positions of the assumed decimal points. Other examples containing the symbols S and V are: S999V9, V999, SV99, 999V. In the last example V is superfluous and can be left out.

We shall now discuss another facility by starting with a simple example. Suppose that we have a variable which can assume numerical values between 0.00000 and 0.00999. Only the last three figures are significant and we want to define an elementary item of corresponding size. The decimal point is situated two positions to the left of the most significant digit and this is indicated by two occurrences of the symbol P. Thus each P stands for one assumed decimal position. Using this facility in our example we can write

```
0 3    C  PICTURE  IS  VPP999.
```

If C contains 371 this will hence mean 0.00371. The letter P represents a scaling position and it is not counted in the size of the data item. The size of C is thus 3 character positions. In a similar way we can use the symbol P to indicate that the assumed decimal point lies to the right of the number contained in the elementary item. Hence, in the example

```
0 3    D  PICTURE  IS  99P(5)V.
```

the contents 01 in D represent the value 100000. Since the presence of a P presupposes an assumed decimal point, the symbol V can be omitted. Our two examples can then be written:

```
0 3    C  PICTURE  PP999.
0 3    D  PICTURE  IS  99P(5).
```

Further examples containing the symbol P are: SVPPP99, S99PP, 999P(6), 99PV, SPPP99.

We have now treated symbols for description of numeric elementary items. It should be mentioned that the COBOL report states that such an item must not contain more than 18 digits (including those indicated by

69

P). However, this limit varies between different computers, and the COBOL manual of the system in question should be consulted.

The picture of a nonedited *alphabetic* elementary item is a sequence of A:s corresponding to the size of the item. Examples:

```
0 2    A  PICTURE  AAA.
0 2    NAME  PICTURE  A(20).
0 2    G  PICTURE  A.
```

Nonedited *alphanumeric* elementary items are specified in the picture as a sequence of X:s corresponding to the size of the item. Examples:

```
0 7    SYMBOL  PICTURE  IS  X.
0 7    MAILING-ADDRESS  PICTURE  IS  X(24).
0 7    SECRET-CODE  PICTURE  IS  XXXXXX.
```

We can also describe alphanumeric elementary items by combining the symbols 9, A and X. This representation can be used to stress the structure of certain alphanumeric data. If we write

```
0 7    SECRET-CODE  PICTURE  IS  AAXA99.
```

we indicate that the elementary item SECRET–CODE begins with two letters and one alphanumeric character and is finished by one letter and two digits. With respect to the program this description is equivalent with the previous one. Every symbol in the picture AAXA99 represents a position which may contain an arbitrary alphanumeric character.

By use of a few additional examples we will try to clarify the meaning of different pictures and how they affect the interpretation of the contents in the corresponding storage areas. In the table below, N stands for numeric, AB for alphabetic, and AN for alphanumeric.

Picture	Category	Size	Contents in the storage area of the elementary item	Used in the procedure division as
9 9 9	N	3	1 2 3	1 2 3
9 9 9 V	N	3	1 2 3	1 2 3
9 9 V 9 9 9	N	5	1 2 3 4 5	1 2 3 4 5
S 9 V 9	N	2	1 2	1 2
V P P 9 9	N	2	1 2	0 0 1 2
9 P	N	1	1	1 0
A A A A	AB	4	A B C D	A B C D
A (1 0)	AB	10	A B C G I J	A B C G I J
A 9	AN	2	A 9	A 9
X	AN	1	P	P

70

In several COBOL systems data transferred to nonnumeric elementary items may contain certain special characters which do not belong to the COBOL characters, e.g. letters in national alphabets. Then provisions have been made for proper reproduction on output.

6.4. Editing

Editing means that data which are to be stored in the storage area of an elementary item are changed according to the picture before the storing is performed. The storing can take place as a result of the verb MOVE or an arithmetic verb. We point out that editing only occurs on the elementary item level. No editing is performed in connection with transfers of groups. The purpose of editing is primarily to give a more attractive shape to data which should be written out in a report than they have in the hardware representation. This is of great importance for readability and for avoiding confusion. The possibility in COBOL to specify editing by the aid of pictures is a concentrated and elegant mode of expression.

If editing is desired when data are transferred to a storage area, this is expressed by one of the 11 editing symbols in the corresponding picture. These symbols are given together with a brief description in the table below.

Symbol	Category of source item	Meaning	Remarks
B	AB, N, AN	Blank	
0	N, AN	Zero	
.	N	Actual decimal point	Corresponds to V in data
Z	N	Zero suppress	
*	N	Check protect	
+	N	Plus	Insertion of + or −
−	N	Minus	Insertion of blank or −
CR	N	Credit sign	Insertion of two blanks or CR
DB	N	Debit sign	Insertion of two blanks or DB
$	N	Currency sign	
,	N	Comma	

In addition to these 11 editing symbols, the 6 general symbols 9, S, V, P, A, and X can also enter the picture.

In order to specify *editing of alphabetic data* we can use the symbol B. In a picture it represents a character position where a blank should be inserted and it is counted when the size of the elementary item is determined. Obviously, the picture must contain at least one A. Examples:

Source item	Size	Picture	Edited result	Size
TWO	3	A A B A	TW O	4
A B	2	A B B A	A B	4
(2 blanks)	2	A A B B	(4 blanks)	4
C D	2	B B A A	C D	4
O S E D	4	A A B A A	O S E D	5

When *alphanumeric* data are edited we can, besides blanks, also insert 0 (zero). This is indicated in the picture by putting 0 in the corresponding position. Both 0 and B are counted when the size of the item is determined. Examples:

Source item	Picture	Edited result
/ 5 H +	X B X X X 0	/ 5 H + 0
9	X 0 0 0	9 0 0 0
+ + +	X B X B X	+ + +
F T	B (3) X X	F T
R –	X X 0 (4)	R – 0 0 0 0

When *numerical data* are edited the symbols in the picture represent not only character positions corresponding to the digits but also positions where an editing symbol is to be inserted. If data contain a fewer number of digits than indicated in the picture, the free space is filled up automatically with zeros to the left and to the right depending on the position of the assumed decimal point. Every editing symbol represents a character in the edited result and must be counted when the size of the elementary item is determined. When numerical data are transferred to an elementary item with editing symbols in its picture by the aid of MOVE or an arithmetic verb, the result will be alphanumeric (except in one case), since the resulting character string will contain other symbols than digits, e.g. plus sign and period. The exception is represented by the case when insertion of zeros is the only editing operation, and then a numerical result is obtained. Contrary to alphanumeric elementary items containing X in the picture, numeric edited elementary items can only receive numerical data.

A period in a picture indicates a position where a decimal point is to be placed. A picture must not contain more than one period which must not appear in the same picture as the symbol V. The period is called an actual decimal point since the character . will be present in the edited result. When the decimal point is inserted the position of the assumed decimal point in the data to be edited is automatically taken into account. Examples:

Source item	Picture	Edited result
1 2 3 4 5	9 9 . 9 9 9	1 2 . 3 4 5
3 4 5	9 . 9 9 9 9	3 . 4 5 0 0
0 3 4 5	9 9 . 9 9	3 4 . 5 0
1 3 4	9 9 9 9 . 9 9	0 0 0 1 . 3 4
0	9 9 . 9	0 0 . 0

In order to bring about a readable print-out leading integer zeros are often replaced by blanks and this is indicated in the picture by the letter Z. In other cases, e.g. in connection with printing amounts of money on checks and other payment documents, we desire to replace the zeros by asterisks for protection purposes. In this case the editing symbol * is used. Since the rules for writing Z in a picture are the same as for * , and since the editing in both cases is about the same, we treat these editing possibilities together. However, it should be observed that Z and * must not occur simultaneously in the same picture; this is quite natural since the symbols are associated with opposite activities. They must represent the leftmost numeric character positions of a picture, i.e. the symbol 9 must not precede the symbol Z or the symbol * . As soon as such a symbol is present in the picture to the right of an actual or assumed decimal point, no symbol 9 is allowed to occur. If Z or * occurs only to the left of the decimal point, then every leading zero, corresponding to Z or * in the picture, is replaced by a blank or an asterisk respectively. This goes on until either a decimal point or the first digit not equal to zero is encountered. If all numeric positions in the picture are indicated by Z or * and the value under consideration is not zero, then the result of the editing will be the same as if the symbols only occurred to the left of the decimal point. If on the other hand the value is zero, then only blanks or only asterisks will be stored in the elementary item, the actual decimal point being left unchanged in the latter case. Note that a V will not give a decimal point in the edited result. Examples:

Source item	Picture	Edited result
0 0 1 0 2	Z Z Z 9 9	1 0 2
0 0 0 0 4	Z Z Z 9 9	0 4
1 2 3 4 5	Z Z Z 9 9	1 2 3 4 5
0 0 1 0 3 4	Z (4) . 9 9	1 0 . 3 4
0 0 0	Z (3) . Z Z	(6 blanks)
0 0 2	Z (3) . Z Z	. 0 2
9	Z (3) . Z Z	9 . 0 0

Source item	Picture	Edited result
1̬ 2 3	Z Z V 9 9	1 2 3
0̬ 8	Z Z V Z Z	0 8
0̬	Z Z V Z Z	(4 blanks)
1 0 2̬	* * * 9 9	* * 1 0 2
2̬	* * * 9 9	* * * 0 2
3 8 0 0̬	* (5) . 9 9	* 3 8 0 0 . 0 0
4̬ 1	* (5) . 9 9	* * * * * . 4 1
0̬	* * * . * *	* * * . * *
1 2 3̬	* * * . * *	1 2 3 . 0 0
9̬	* * * . * *	* * 9 . 0 0
0̬ 9	* * * . * *	* * * . 0 9
1̬ 2 3	* * V 9 9	* 1 2 3
0 0̬ 0 8	* * V * *	* * 0 8
0̬	* * V * *	* * * *
0 0 8̬	* * * *	* * * 8
3 1 0 0̬	* (3) 9 (3) . 9 9	* * 3 1 0 0 . 0 0
1 2̬3	* (3) 9 (3) . 9 9	* * * 0 1 2 . 3 0
0̬ 0 0 0 0 0 0 7	P (4) Z (4)	0 0 0 7
0̬	P (4) * (4)	* * * *
6 2 7 0 0 0̬ 0 0	Z (4) P (3)	6 2 7

In Section 6.3. we defined the operational sign. Since it does not occupy a special character position its value will not appear on print-out unless editing is performed first. We shall now describe different ways to specify the sign in a numeric edited elementary item. Since the rules for insertion of a currency symbol are similar, this kind of editing will be treated in parallel. The edited equivalent of an operational sign is called an *edited sign control character*. The insertion of such a character or a currency symbol can be either *fixed* or *floating*. In the first case we define through the picture a unique position where the insertion should take place. In the second case the position is determined by the picture and by the form of the source item.

The symbols +, −, CR, and DB are used to indicate the position where the edited sign control character is to be placed. Such a symbol must not appear more than once in a picture if *fixed insertion* is desired. The symbols + and − must be placed in the picture in such a way that the edited sign control character comes to the far left or to the far right in the edited result. If the editing symbol is + the result is that a plus sign appears if the operational sign is positive or no operational sign is present; otherwise a minus sign is inserted. If the editing symbol is − we have the same rules with the exception that the plus sign is replaced by a blank. Examples:

Source item	Picture	Edited result
1 2 3 $\overset{+}{4}$	9 9 9 9 +	1 2 3 4 +
1 2 3 $\overset{-}{4}$	9 9 9 9 +	1 2 3 4 -
1 2 3 4	9 9 9 9 +	1 2 3 4 +
1 2 3 $\overset{-}{4}$	9 9 9 -	1 2 3 4 -
1 2 3 $\overset{+}{4}$	- 9 9 9 9	1 2 3 4
1 2 3 $\overset{-}{4}$	- 9 9 9 9	- 1 2 3 4
1 2 3 4	- 9 9 9 9	1 2 3 4
1 2 3 $\overset{+}{4}$	+ 9 9 9 9	+ 1 2 3 4

The symbols CR and DB must occur to the right in the picture and may be followed only by the symbol P. Both CR and DB represent two character positions. If the numerical value is positive or has no operational sign two blanks are inserted, if the value is negative the symbol CR or DB is inserted, whichever is used in the picture. Examples:

Source item	Picture	Edited result
1 2 3 $\overset{+}{4}$	9 9 9 9 CR	1 2 3 4
1 2 3 4	9 9 9 9 DB	1 2 3 4
1 2 3 $\overset{-}{4}$	9 9 9 9 CR	1 2 3 4 CR
1 2 3 $\overset{-}{4}$	9 9 9 9 DB	1 2 3 4 DB

The currency symbol is specified by the implementor of the COBOL system used. In this book we use the dollar sign. When used as a fixed insertion symbol in the picture it must not be preceded by any other symbol representing a character position than + or −. As a result of the editing a currency symbol is inserted into the position specified in the picture. Examples of fixed insertion:

Source item	Picture	Edited result
1 2 3	$ 9 . 9 9	$ 1 . 2 3
9 9 9 9	+ $ 9 9 . 9 9	+ $ 9 9 . 9 9
9 9 $\overline{9}$	+ $ 9 9 . 9 9	− $ 0 9 . 9 9
0	+ Z Z Z . Z Z	(7 blanks)
1 5 1	+ Z Z Z . Z Z	+ 1 5 . 1 0
1 2 3	+ Z Z Z . Z Z	+ 1 . 2 3

Source item	Picture	Edited result
1 1 5	* * * . * * +	* * 1 . 1 5 +
0	* * * . * * +	* * * . * * *
3 1 4 1 6	Z (4) . Z (4) −	3 . 1 4 1 6
2 7 8̄	Z (4) . Z (4) −	2 . 7 8 0 0 −
1 0 5 6 4̄	Z Z 9 9 . 9 9 C R	1 0 5 . 6 4 C R
7 1 2̄	* * 9 9 . 9 9 D B	* * 0 7 . 1 2 D B
1 2 3̄	Z Z Z 9 . 9 9 C R	1 2 . 3 0
1 2 3	Z Z Z 9 . 9 9 D B	1 2 . 3 0
3 8 0 0̄	9 9 9 D B P P	0 3 8 D B
0 0 0 0 1 2	P P P Z Z Z −	0 1 2
0 0 0 0 3 4̄	P P P Z Z Z −	0 3 4 −
4	− Z Z Z 9	4
4̄	− Z Z Z 9	− 4
1 0 0 0 0	9 9 + P P P	1 0 +
9 8 4 9̄	$ * * * . * * C R	$ * 9 8 . 4 9 C R
0	$ * * * . * * C R	* * * * . * * * *

Floating insertion can be described simplest as suppression of leading zeros in data, the last of these zeros being replaced by an edited sign control character or a currency symbol instead of a blank. This technique is used in order to avoid blanks between +, −, or $ and the first digit which is not suppressed in a print-out. Floating insertion is indicated in a picture by a sequence of at least two symbols +, −, or $ representing the numeric positions to the far left in the picture. Since one position is always used for insertion of the desired symbol, the floating symbols in the picture must be at least one more than the number of digits which they are intended to represent. For example, the picture +++99 is designed for editing of data consisting of at most four integer digits. If a floating symbol stands to the right of an assumed or actual decimal point, it must appear in all digit positions of the picture. If floating symbols are present only to the left of the decimal point the result of the editing will be as follows. An insertion symbol is placed in the character position represented in the picture by a floating symbol, immediately before the first digit not equal to zero or the decimal point, whichever is first encountered. Zeros in data preceding this very position are replaced by blanks. If all numeric character positions are represented by floating symbols and the value of the source item is zero, then the edited result will contain only blanks. If on the other hand the value of the source item is different from zero, the editing is performed exactly as if floating symbols were present only to the left of the decimal point. Examples:

Source item	Picture	Edited result
0 1 2 3	+ + + 9 9	+ 1 2 3
1 1 4 7̄ +	+ + + 9 9	- 1 1 4 7
7	+ + + 9 9	+ 0 7
1 3	- - - - -	1 3
0 0 0 1̄	- - - - -	- 1
0 0 1 +	+ + + . + +	+ . 0 1
0 0 1 +	- - - . - -	. 0 1
0	- - - . - -	(6 blanks)
0 6 7 9	$ $ $ 9 9	$ 6 7 9
7	$ $ $ 9 9	$ 0 7
0	$ $ $. $ $	(6 blanks)
0 0 4	$ $ $. $ $	$. 0 4
0 0 4	$ $ 9 . 9 9	$ 0 . 0 4
0 0 1	$ $ $ $	$ 1

Zero suppression and floating insertion must not occur in the same picture, i.e. Z and * are not allowed to be present in a picture containing floating symbols. When the floating symbol is a currency symbol, fixed insertion of an edited sign control character may occur, and when the floating symbol is + or −, the picture may contain a fixed currency symbol. Examples:

Source item	Picture	Edited result
0 0 7 1 2 5	$ + + + + + . + +	$ + 7 1 . 2 5
2 1 5 0	+ $ $ $ $. 9 9	− $ 2 1 . 5 0
2 2 0 0 0̄ +	$ $ $ C R P P P	$ 2 2 C R
0 2 1 5 0	− $ $ $ 9 . 9 9	$ 2 1 . 5 0

The symbols B, 0 (zero), and , (comma) in the picture represent positions where a blank, a zero, or a comma are to be inserted. Examples:

Source item	Picture	Edited result
1 7 6	9 9 9 0 0 0	1 7 6 0 0 0
1 2 3	S 9 0 0 9 9	1 0 0 2 3̄
0 1 2 3 4 5	9 9 B B 9 9 B B 9 9	0 1 2 3 4 5
1 2 3 4 5 6	9 9 , B 9 9 , B 9 9	1 2 , 3 4 , 5 6
1 1 2 7 6 1	9 9 9 , 9 9 9 . 9 9	0 0 1 , 1 2 7 . 6 1
5 3	9 , (5) 9	5 , , , , , 3
3 7 4	9 B (6) 9 9	3 7 4

Note that the edited result in the first two examples becomes numeric. If the insertion symbols B, 0 (zero), or , (comma) occur together with Z, *, or floating symbols, then special rules are valid. Every B, 0, or , (comma) which is present inside or immediately after the string of such symbols is interpreted as part of this string. Examples:

Source item	Picture	Edited result
0 0 0 1 2̬8 1	* *, * *, * . 9 9	* * * * 1 , 2 . 8 1
1 2 3 4 5̬6 7	* *, * *, * . 9 9	1 2 , 3 4 , 5 . 6 7
7 8̅ ̬	+ Z , Z , 9 9 . 9	− 7 8 . 0
4 ̬	Z Z 0 0 Z	4
2 1 ̬	Z Z 0 0 Z	2 0 0 1
5 1 2̬4 3	+ + + + , + + + . + +	+ 5 1 2 . 4 3
1 1 9 7̬5 1̅	− − − − , − − − . − −	− 1 , 1 9 7 . 5 1
7 1 4̬1 9	$ $, $ $ $. $ $	$ 7 1 4 . 1 9
5 3 7̬2	+ + + + , B 9 9 . 9 9	+ 5 3 . 7 2

6.5. Further options to specify storing

In connection with the description of the verb MOVE (5.3.) a few rules were given for storing data in a storage area. In the Sections 6.3. and 6.4. we have seen how the description of the receiving elementary item affects the data to be stored. Normally we have the same rules if data are fetched from a storage area by a MOVE-statement or appear as the result of an arithmetic operation. In this section we shall consider some cases of storing which have not been treated before, as well as some further options to specify a storing process. We shall also briefly discuss how we can affect the efficiency of a COBOL program by some simple measures.

Whenever data are stored in the storage area of an elementary item it must be observed that the form of the data and the description of the item are not in conflict with each other. Alphabetic data, of course, can be transferred to alphanumeric elementary items. The reverse transfer, however, is allowed only if the alphanumeric item consists of letters and blanks exclusively. Further, it is not possible to move a numeric edited item (which as a matter of fact is alphanumeric) to a numeric or alphabetic elementary item.

By use of a few examples we shall illustrate how a numerical data item is modified when it is transferred to an elementary item with a picture which does not completely coincide with the form or the source item. The transfer in the last two examples is supposed to occur by a MOVE-statement (cf. 5.4.).

Source item	Picture of receiving elementary item	Contents after storing
1 2	9 9 9 V 9 9	0 0 1 2 0
3 4 5 6 7	9 V 9 9 9	3 4 5 6
1 0	9 9	1 0
1 2 3	9 9	2 3
1 2 3	9 9 V 9 9	2 3 0 0

Note that the incongruity of the source item and the picture in the last three examples causes a misrepresentation on storing.

As has been mentioned earlier storing of data is performed from left to right in alphabetic and alphanumeric elementary items. By use of the clause JUSTIFIED RIGHT in the description of such elementary items we can achieve storing of the characters from right to left. Examples:

Source item	Picture of receiving elementary item	Type of storing	Contents after storing
A B L E	A (7)	normal	A B L E
A B L E	A (7)	justified right	A B L E
B A K E R	X X X	normal	B A K
B A K E R	X X X	justified right	K E R

It should also be pointed out here that when a data item, consisting of a group of elementary items, is involved in a transfer, this is performed in the same way as an alphanumeric—alphanumeric transfer, i.e. storing takes place character by character in the receiving storage area. In this case there is no editing or other conversion whatsoever between different representations. Note that an editing symbol then corresponds to a character position.

In cases when the COBOL system allows more than one representation of data in the internal storage of the computer, the programmer can indicate the main use of the data item by the aid of the clause

$$\text{USAGE IS} \left\{ \frac{\text{COMPUTATIONAL}}{\text{DISPLAY}} \right\}$$

to guarantee a suitable representation. The alternative COMPUTATIONAL is used for numeric elementary items and indicates that a representation appropriate for numerical computations should be applied, while DISPLAY indicates a representation convenient for print-out. The clause may be written on an arbitrary level. When it appears on group level it refers to all subordinate elementary items. If an elementary item and its superior groups do not have the USAGE-clause, this means that a representation corresponding to USAGE IS DISPLAY will be chosen automatically. The clause does not imply any restrictions in the use of a data item. Thus, a numeric elementary item with the clause USAGE IS DISPLAY can also be used in numerical computations, but the effect may be considerably slower object programs.

In word organized computers, as a rule, consecutive elementary items are placed in successive character positions without taking the word structure into account. For this reason a word may contain several elementary items, and an elementary item may occupy several words. This way of storing implies an effective use of the memory, but on the other hand fetching and storing information may become rather time-consuming. For elementary items often referred to in the program we can then use the clause

$$\underline{\text{SYNCHRONIZED}} \left\{ \frac{\underline{\text{LEFT}}}{\underline{\text{RIGHT}}} \right\}$$

with the effect that the elementary item is placed in the least possible number of words in the memory. Character positions which are possibly left in such a machine word are not used by other elementary items. The alternative LEFT means that the item is stored with the first character in the position to the left in the reserved area, the alternative RIGHT having an obvious analogous meaning. The clause may be specified only for elementary items. Under what circumstances this clause is advantageous to use is described in the COBOL manual for the system in question. Each system manual will also specify how groups containing an elementary item with the clause SYNCHRONIZED are treated. Often subscripted items (described in 6.6.) are given this clause implying quicker computation of their addresses in the memory. We emphasize that the clause is machine dependent and has no meaning in many COBOL systems.

6.6. Subscripting

When large amounts of data with the same structure have to be treated subscripting is often very convenient. One advantage is that we do not have to introduce a great many data-names, another that the general structure can be surveyed in a much more clear way. In particular, this is the case for tables with several rows and columns.

For the reasons mentioned there exists a possibility in COBOL to use subscripted data-names; however, the number of subscripts is limited to three. Obviously, special arrangements are required primarily in the data division, but to some extent also in the procedure division. Subscripted

80

data-names are defined by the clause OCCURS which can be constructed in two different ways:

$$\underline{\text{OCCURS}} \begin{cases} \text{integer-1 TIMES} \\ \text{integer-2 } \underline{\text{TO}} \text{ integer-3 TIMES [}\underline{\text{DEPENDING ON}} \text{ data-name]} \end{cases}$$

The key word OCCURS must not be present on the 01-level, neither on the 77-level.

We now suppose that we need a table of the number of employees in the government of the kingdom Idyllia. There are altogether 15 departments, viz.

1. Ballistics	6. Atomics	11. Weather
2. Boxing	7. Administration	12. Geometry
3. Comics	8. Commercials	13. Truth
4. Cosmetics	9. Culture	14. Love
5. Cosmology	10. Conformity	15. Flowerpower

We could, of course, introduce 15 different data-names, BALLISTICS, ..., FLOWERPOWER, but it is simpler to define in the data division a table with 15 entries as follows.

```
0 1    EXPERT-TABLE.
    0 2    EXPERT PICTURE 9999 OCCURS 15 TIMES.
```

Now, EXPERT (1) refers to ballistics, EXPERT (2) to boxing, and so on. If 23 new experts on commercials are appointed, this can be expressed in the procedure division through the statement:

```
ADD 23 TO EXPERT (8)
```

It should be observed that we must have a blank before the left parenthesis. On the other hand, blanks are not allowed between either of the parentheses and the subscript.

Now suppose that each department consists of 16 divisions:

1. Constitutions	9. Directions
2. Laws	10. Precepts
3. Statutes	11. Instructions
4. Regulations	12. Public investigations
5. General rules	13. Secret investigations
6. Special rules	14. Orders
7. Edicts	15. Commands
8. Decrees	16. Espionage

Finally, we suppose that every division has employees of the following categories:

1. President
2. Vice president
3. Chancellor
4. Treasurer
5. Systems consultant
6. Chief programmer

7. Programmer
8. Operator
9. Chief secretary
10. Secretary
11. Engineer
12. Doorman

In the data division we could define the table like this:

```
01    EXPERT-TABLE.
      02    EXPERT OCCURS 15 TIMES.
            03    DEPT-EXPERT OCCURS 16 TIMES.
                  04 DIV-EXPERT PICTURE 9999
                     OCCURS 12 TIMES.
```

Then e.g. DIV – EXPERT (11, 13, 7) indicates the number of programmers working on secret investigations within the weather department. Commas, followed by blanks, are compulsory in a sequence of subscripts. We can also refer to a higher level, for example DEPT – EXPERT (12, 2) giving the set (not the sum!) of the number of employees of all categories working with laws of geometry within the government. In our case the set consists of 12 numeric elementary items. Obviously, the subscripts always go from 1 upwards.

It should also be observed that a subscripted data item may contain other data items, with or without an OCCURS-clause. If in the preceding example we want to emphasize the position of the president, we can modify the data description as follows:

```
01    EXPERT-TABLE.
      02    EXPERT OCCURS 15 TIMES.
            03    DEPT-EXPERT OCCURS 16 TIMES.
                  04 PRESIDENT PICTURE 9999.
                  04 DIV-EXPERT PICTURE 9999
                     OCCURS 11 TIMES.
```

Items not containing an OCCURS-clause are identified with the same subscripts as the nearest superior subscripted group, and PRESIDENT (2, 6) is obviously the number of presidents working with special rules for boxing within the government.

We shall also discuss the alternative construction. Suppose that we have a table called PRICE – LIST which is known to contain at least 25 and at most 150 elements. We can indicate this by writing

```
01    PRICE-LIST.
      02 PRICE PICTURE 9999V99
         OCCURS 25 TO 150 TIMES.
```

Often one wants to define the actual number by the aid of some quantity contained in the program. In such cases a clause of the form DEPENDING ON ITEM – TOTAL can be added. The quantity ITEM – TOTAL then must have a value between 25 and 150, both limits inclusive.

If subscripted data-names are used in the procedure division, the subscript must be a numeric literal or a data-name which is not subscripted. The value of the subscript must always be an integer > 0. If we work with quantities belonging to a certain hierarchy this is indicated in the usual way by qualified data-names. The same rule applies also to subscripts. Hence we can write e.g.

PRICE IN PRICE–LIST (ITEM IN MASTER)

and similar constructions are allowed also when several subscripts are present.

6.7. Description of files

In the environment division to be described in Section 7.1. one or more external units are assigned to every file, and in this way the storage medium of the file is determined. Certain types of media allow for different ways of recording data. A suitable way can then be chosen according to the contents of the file. This must then be indicated in the file section of the data division by the aid of a number of clauses in the file description entry. As has been mentioned previously (cf. 6.1.) a file description entry is followed by record descriptions, one for each kind of record in the file.

Moreover, in the file description entry the type of the records contained in the file must be stated. The records may constitute either data records or label records. The *data records* are the proper objects of the program to be treated in the procedure division. The *label records* contain special characteristics of the file and they are stored in suitable areas of the storage medium, e.g. at the beginning or at the end of a file stored on magnetic tape, or at the physical ends of the tape. The function of the label records is usually of a standard character. The handling is attended automatically by a supervising machine program consisting of a set of input-output procedures which is fit into the object program on compilation. This handling takes place on certain special occasions, e.g. when a file is opened or closed, or when the processing has reached the beginning or the end of a magnetic tape. For output files the label records are stored with contents which have either been indicated in the file description entry or have been automatically formed by the supervising program. For input files the same label records are tested against the corresponding values. Each

COBOL system has *standard label records,* the treatment of which has been completely specified by the implementor. No record description is needed in a COBOL program for such label records. However, in some COBOL systems it is also permissible to form label records of one's own, specified in an ordinary record description, and then treat them accordingly. Their function and treatment must then be indicated in a section of the procedure division under the header DECLARATIVES. This section is then connected with the input-output system by the aid of the verb USE. This possibility will be treated in more detail in Section 9.2.

A file description entry has essentially the following format. Further clauses may be attached, but for details in this respect we must refer to the system manuals.

FD file-name

[; RECORDING MODE IS mode]

$$\left[; \text{BLOCK CONTAINS integer} \left\{\begin{array}{l}\underline{\text{RECORDS}} \\ \underline{\text{CHARACTERS}}\end{array}\right\}\right]$$

$$; \text{LABEL} \left\{\begin{array}{l}\underline{\text{RECORDS}} \text{ ARE} \\ \underline{\text{RECORD}} \text{ IS}\end{array}\right\} \left\{\begin{array}{l}\underline{\text{OMITTED}} \\ \underline{\text{STANDARD}} \\ \text{data-name-1 [, data-name2]} \dots\end{array}\right\}$$

$$\left[; \text{VALUE OF data-name-in-label-record-1 IS} \left\{\begin{array}{l}\text{data-name-3} \\ \text{literal-1}\end{array}\right\}\right.$$

$$\left.\text{[, data-name-in-label-record-2 IS} \left\{\begin{array}{l}\text{data-name-4} \\ \text{literal-2}\end{array}\right\}] \dots\right]$$

$$; \text{DATA} \left\{\begin{array}{l}\underline{\text{RECORDS}} \text{ ARE} \\ \underline{\text{RECORD}} \text{ IS}\end{array}\right\} \text{data-name-5 [, data-name-6]} \dots .$$

A file description entry starts with the level indicator FD (= File Description) and the name of the file which is a data-name, and is terminated by a period. The essential contents are formed according to the format above, and we shall now describe the different clauses.

If there are several ways of recording data on a certain external medium, one of these can be chosen through the following clause:

RECORDING MODE IS mode

The mode corresponds to different possibilities defined by the implementor. There are e.g. magnetic tapes with different recording densities. If in a certain COBOL system we have the alternatives DENSITY – 1, DENSITY – 2, ... the clause could have the form

RECORDING MODE IS DENSITY-2

84

The following clause is related to conventional magnetic tape equipment:

$$\underline{\text{BLOCK}} \text{ CONTAINS integer} \left\{ \frac{\text{RECORDS}}{\text{CHARACTERS}} \right\}$$

Data are stored in blocks (cf. 2.4.), and after each block there is a rather long gap on the tape. A machine instruction for reading will transfer a whole block from tape to an area in the internal storage. However, on transfers from the internal storage to tape the block size can be chosen arbitrarily. The READ- and WRITE-instructions of COBOL will operate on one record at a time. The records are groups of data collected on logical decisions, and from this point of view it seems natural to store every single record as a block. However, this technique might mean a waste of tape space and of time since the conventional tape units for mechanical reasons need a fairly long initializing period in connection with each transfer. The clause gives us a possibility to save space and time by grouping together a number of records to blocks of suitable size, or by forming suitable units for transfer in some other way. The READ- and WRITE-instructions will then in practice imply references to buffer areas with periodically recurring tape operations. The integer in the format above states the number of records or characters contained in a block. The option of giving the number of characters need only be applied when the number of records cannot be used which is highly dependent on the equipment available. It should be observed that the word CHARACTERS may be omitted. The block length concept can be given a meaning also for other kinds of storage media. For example, in a punched cards file every card can be considered as a block. However, since it has a fixed length, the clause is unnecessary.

Label records are specified in clauses with the format:

$$\underline{\text{LABEL}} \left\{ \frac{\text{RECORDS}}{\text{RECORD}} \text{ ARE} \atop \text{IS} \right\} \left\{ \frac{\text{OMITTED}}{\text{STANDARD}} \atop \text{data-name-1 [, data-name-2]} \ldots \right\}$$

$$\left[; \underline{\text{VALUE}} \underline{\text{OF}} \text{ data-name-in-label-record-1 IS} \left\{ \text{data-name-3} \atop \text{literal-1} \right\} \right.$$

$$\left. [, \text{ data-name-in-label-record-2 IS} \left\{ \text{data-name-4} \atop \text{literal-2} \right\}] \ldots \right]$$

A file may contain label records of different kinds, or it may lack such records completely. This matter must be specified in the first clause. RECORDS ARE and RECORD IS are equivalent. OMITTED means that no label records are present in the file, and if so the second clause will not be used. STANDARD means that the file is supposed to have standard label records. In this case the input-output procedures will automatically treat the contents of the records which consist of control sums and other elements of importance for a correct handling of the file on reading and writing. Obvious examples are record and block tallies or tape numbers in cases when a file occupies several tapes. Certain data items in the label records are symbolized by implementor-names, and for output files they obtain values which can be specified in the VALUE OF-clause. For input files the contents of the data items are tested automatically. The elements data-name-1, data-name-2, and so on in the first clause symbolize the programmer's own label records which must be explained in subsequent record descriptions. Also in this case values chosen by the programmer may be assigned to data items in these records by use of the VALUE OF-clause.

Data records are specified in a clause with the format:

$$\text{DATA} \left\{ \begin{array}{l} \underline{\text{RECORDS}} \text{ ARE} \\ \underline{\text{RECORD}} \text{ IS} \end{array} \right\} \text{data-name-5 [, data-name-6]} \ldots$$

This clause must not be omitted and is supposed to contain an enumeration of the data records appearing in the record descriptions of the file. For every file an area is reserved in the internal storage, and here the records of the file are processed. This area is the same for all records in the file irrespective of the fact that it may contain several kinds of records. For this reason the records must be treated one at a time.

Finally, we give an example of a file description.

```
FD    I-FILE; RECORDING MODE IS HIGH-DENSITY;
      BLOCK CONTAINS 10 RECORDS; LABEL RECORD
      IS STANDARD;
      VALUE OF ID IS "INVOICES"; DATA RECORDS
      ARE ADDR, ITEM.
01    ADDR.
      02 I-NO PICTURE 9(5).
      02 RECORD-TYPE PICTURE X.
      02 NAME ...
      .
      .
      .
01    ITEM.
      02 I-NO PICTURE 9(5).
      02 RECORD-TYPE PICTURE X.
      02 ARTICLE ...
      .
      .
      .
```

In this example, we have supposed that the computer has conventional magnetic tapes with two different recording densities called HIGH-DENSITY and LOW-DENSITY in the COBOL system for this computer. Further we have assumed that the system also offers a kind of standard label record containing the elementary item ID which should always be given a value by the programmer through the VALUE OF-clause. The file which is being processed contains material for production of invoices and is supposed to be stored with high density and 10 records in each block. The file starts with the standard label record where ID has the value "INVOICES". Every invoice should consist of an address and some further details, and these data are assembled in two kinds of records in the file, ADDR and ITEM. The records are assumed to be sorted first on invoice number (I – NO) and secondly on record type so that they are collected invoice by invoice with the address record first.

6.8. Working-storage and constants

In the introduction to this chapter we mentioned that data items defining just working-storage in the internal memory of the computer must be specified in the working-storage section. Hierarchies of data are described in record descriptions where the highest level as usual is represented by the level number 01. Further noncontiguous elementary item entries may occur with the following form:

```
7 7    L I NE - TA LLY   P I C T U R E   9 9 .
```

The level number 77 indicates that the elementary item is completely independent of other data items. All specifications of noncontiguous elementary items must occur before the record descriptions of the section. In other respects these elementary items are described in the usual way.

On the description of data items in the working-storage section we can also use a clause with the format:

VALUE IS literal

Examples of entries with such clauses:

```
7 7    L I NE - TA LLY   P I C T U R E   9 9   VALUE   IS   1 .
0 3    H E A D I NG - 3   P I C T U R E   X ( 4 )   VALUE   "ONE" .
0 3    S T R I NG   P I C T U R E   X ( 8 0 )   VALUE   IS   SPACES .
```

By this clause the data item obtains a starting value valid for the item when the object program starts. If there is no such clause, there is also no starting value. Instead, such a value must be assigned in the procedure division, e.g. by a MOVE-statement. When the program stores a new value into the data item, the initial value is, of course, destroyed. There are certain rules relating to the use of the VALUE-clause. If the data item to be described is a numeric elementary item, the literal must be numeric, and corresponding rules are valid for alphabetic and alphanumeric elementary items. The size of a literal must lie within the limits indicated by the picture of the data item. When stored, a numeric literal will be automatically adjusted according to the assumed decimal point in the picture if the number of decimals in the literal is less than or equal to the number of decimals in the picture. Literals with an excess of decimals must not occur. Nonnumeric literals of smaller length than the corresponding picture, are stored in a conventional way from left to right, with blanks to the far right. If a picture contains editing symbols, these do not imply editing on initiation with VALUE but only determine a character position. For example, PICTURE ZZ.99 in this respect has the same meaning as PICTURE X(5), and the literal following VALUE must be nonnumeric.

If the VALUE-clause occurs on group level the literal must be a figurative constant or a nonnumeric literal. It is stored character by character in the area reserved for the group, without taking into account the further subdivision of the group into data items. No new VALUE-clauses may occur on these lower levels. For subscripted variables the VALUE-clause has no meaning.

In the introduction to this chapter we also introduced the constant section. The purpose of this section is to give names to constants. The constant section is organized in exactly the same way as the working-storage section, but each data item has to be initiated by a VALUE-clause.

6.9. Example

We conclude this chapter with an example of a complete data division containing three file descriptions.

```
DATA DIVISION.
FILE SECTION.
FD   OLD-REG; LABEL RECORD STANDARD;
     VALUE OF ID IS "1966";
     DATA RECORD IS TOWNSHIP.
01   TOWNSHIP.
     02   COUNTY PICTURE AA.
     02   NAME PICTURE X(24).
     02   CATEGORY PICTURE 9.
     02   POPULATION PICTURE 9(7).
     02   TAX-RATE PICTURE 99V99.
FD   NEW-REG; LABEL RECORD STANDARD;
     VALUE OF ID IS "1967";
     DATA RECORD IS TOWNSHIP.
01   TOWNSHIP.
     02   COUNTY PICTURE AA.
     02   NAME PICTURE X(24).
     02   CATEGORY PICTURE 9.
     02   POPULATION PICTURE 9(7).
     02   TAX-RATE PICTURE 99V99.
FD   TABLE; LABEL RECORDS OMITTED;
     DATA RECORDS ARE HEADER, TOWNSHIP, TOTAL.
01   HEADER.
     02   TEXT PICTURE X(10).
     02   COUNTY PICTURE AA.
```

```
0 1   TOWNSHIP .
      0 2   NAME  PICTURE  X ( 2 4 ) .
      0 2   POPULATION  PICTURE  Z ( 8 ) .
      0 2   POP-INCREASE  + ( 6 ) 9 .
      0 2   TAX-RATE  PICTURE  Z ( 8 ) . 9 9 .
      0 2   TAX-INCREASE  + ( 8 ) . 9 9 .
0 1   TOTAL .
      0 2   TEXT  PICTURE  X ( 2 4 ) .
      0 2   POPULATION-SUMS .
            0 3   POP-TOTAL  PICTURE  Z ( 8 ) .
            0 3   DIFF-TOTAL  PICTURE  + ( 7 ) 9 .
            0 3   POP-CITY  PICTURE  Z ( 8 ) .
            0 3   DIFF-CITY  PICTURE  + ( 7 ) 9 .
            0 3   POP-COUNTRY  PICTURE  Z ( 8 ) .
            0 3   DIFF-COUNTRY  PICTURE  + ( 7 ) 9 .
WORKING-STORAGE  SECTION .
7 7   CURR-COUNTY  PICTURE  AA .
7 7   DIFF  PICTURE  9 ( 7 ) .
0 1   PART-SUMS .
      0 3   POP-TOTAL  PICTURE  9 ( 7 ) .
      0 3   DIFF-TOTAL  PICTURE  S 9 ( 6 ) .
      0 3   POP-CITY  PICTURE  9 ( 7 ) .
      0 3   DIFF-CITY  PICTURE  S 9 ( 6 ) .
      0 3   POP-COUNTRY  PICTURE  9 ( 7 ) .
      0 3   DIFF-COUNTRY  PICTURE  S 9 ( 6 ) .
```

We assume that every year a register is constructed for the townships of a state with respect to population and tax. The townships are identified through the county and the name, and they are supposed to be sorted on these arguments in turn. A special code indicates the category (city, country) to which the township belongs. The described data division is intended for a COBOL program with the following task. Starting from the registers of the last two years with identical file descriptions, the values for the last year together with the differences compared with the preceding year will be written out. Further, for each county we want the total population and the change in population written out as well as the corresponding data for different categories. The print-out is composed of three different records, one heading for each county, one giving data for a certain township, and one giving the county-total of the population. The pictures of the different data items contain editing symbols aiming at a readable print-out. They have been chosen in such a way that the print-out of an elementary item always starts with a number of blanks.

In the working-storage section there are two noncontiguous elements, one indicator for the current county, and one auxiliary variable for a difference which has just been computed. Further, in the record PART–SUMS we have brought together a number of elementary items where populations and differences in population are accumulated. The dividing in elementary items has a direct counterpart in the group POPULATION–SUMS in the record TOTAL of the file TABLE. Before TOTAL is written out the contents of PART–SUMS must be moved to POPULATION–SUMS. From what we know so far with respect to the verb MOVE this must be done with eight elementary transfers because each elementary item must be edited. Hence the formation of groups may seem unnecessary disregarding the increased readability of the program. However, in Section 9.2. we shall describe a more advanced technique (MOVE CORRESPONDING) to perform transfers on group level. If this facility has been implemented on the computer there is a good reason for forming groups as indicated above.

Exercises

1. Giving level numbers, describe the structure of the record SALARY–SPECIFICATION illustrated below:

SALARY–SPECIFICATION											
EMP–NO	NAME	ADDR	TO–DATE		EMOLUMENTS			DEDUCTIONS			NET–PAY
								TAXES			
			PREL–TAX	GROSS–PAY	SA-LARY	FEE	VAR-IOUS	PREL	ARRE-ARS	VAR-IOUS	

2. Illustrate the structure of the record A with braces as in the example TIME–CARD on page 63. How is the structure affected if the level number of H is changed to 04?

0 1	A
0 2	B
0 2	C
0 3	D
0 4	E
0 4	F
0 3	G
0 2	H
0 6	I

3. Find size and category of elementary items containing:

a) 2 7
b) V E F
c) 2 1 $\bar{1}$
d) + 9 6
e) 1 3 $\overset{+}{4}$
f) 1   4 3 6
g) 0 1$_{\wedge}$5
h) 1 2 . 7 4
i) A 4
j) B   C
k) B R . K C
l) – 3 1 . 9 7

4. What will be the result of the statements DISPLAY A, DISPLAY B, DISPLAY C, when A has the value 12345, B 1234$\bar{5}$, and C 123$\overset{+}{4}$5? In the data division the elementary items A, B, and C are described through:

```
0 2    A   PICTURE   9 ( 5 ) .
0 2    B   PICTURE   S 9 ( 5 ) .
0 2    C   PICTURE   S 9 9 9 V 9 9 .
```

5. State size and category for elementary items with contents as given below. Also determine how they are used in the procedure division.

Picture	Contents	Picture	Contents
a) V 9 9 9	1 0 2	j) A X	P .
b) S 9 9 V 9	1 2 3̇	k) X X X	2 . 7
c) 9 (5) P (4) V	1 2 3 4 5	l) X X X X X	+ 1 . 7 6
d) S V P P 9	1̄	m) 9 P V	5
e) S 9 P P P	1̇	n) 9 9 (4) P V	0 0 1 2 3
f) P 9	1	o) S P P 9 (3)	0 0 1̄
g) A (6)	B U S T E R	p) S 9 (3) P P	0 0 1̄
h) X 9 X	B 6)	q) 9 9 A 9 9	1 2 K 2 1
i) X (7)	+ + + - - 0 1	r) A	F

6. Write data description entries for the following elementary items:
   a) JOB – TIME with level number 03. JOB – TIME is a positive four-digit number with 2 decimals.
   b) LOAN with level number 05. LOAN is stored with thousand as unit, has 5 significant figures and can take positive as well as negative values.
   c) COUNTY with level number 02. COUNTY is supposed to contain the name of a county or an abbreviation; size 8 characters.
   d) A with level number 10. A stands for a number with 6 decimals, the first two being zeros, and can assume positive as well as negative values.

7. Give pictures for elementary items intended for the following editings:
   a) Editing of data containing three integer digits and two decimals. The edited result should have a decimal point. Leading zeros are supposed to be replaced by blanks, and the value zero should give blanks only.
   b) Editing of a five-digit integer. If the number starts with one or two zeros, these are to be replaced by blanks.
   c) Editing of data containing seven digits, two of which are decimals. If leading zeros occur, at most three are to be replaced by blanks.
   d) The elementary item PERFORMED – WORK containing two integer digits and two decimals gives the amount of performed work in hours. The contents are to be edited for print-out in hundredths of

hours as unit. Leading integer zeros are to be replaced by asterisks; if the value is zero, all positions should contain asterisks.

8. State the result of the editing if the following values are moved to elementary items with pictures as defined in exercise 7.

a) 9 , 0 1 , 0 , 1 7 8 2 1   (picture as 7a)

b) 0 , 1 1 7 4 , 1 0   (picture as 7b)

c) 9 5 , 0 0 1 0 2 3 1 , 0 , 7 1 0   (picture as 7c)

d) 4 8 3 4 , 1 5 0 0 , 0 0 2 7 , 0 0 0 0 , 0 0 0 5   (picture as 7d)

9. Determine the result of the editing in the examples below (data to the left, picture to the right) :

a) 0 0 2 7   V Z Z Z Z   g) 1 2   ∗ 9 9 9 9 9

b) 0 0 0 0 0   V Z Z Z Z   h) 0 0 7 1 9   Z Z Z V 9 9

c) 0 1 1 3   9 9 . 9 9 9 9   i) 0 2 3 0 9 5 0   Z Z 9 9 . 9 9 9 9

d) 0 0 0 1 1   V ∗ ∗ ∗ ∗   j) 2 1 4 1 2   ∗ ∗ ∗ 9 9 9 . 9 9 9 9

e) 0   ∗ ∗ ∗ ∗ . ∗ ∗   k) 0 3 1   Z . 9 9

f) 1 2   ∗ 9 9 9 V 9 9   l) 0 3 1   ∗ . ∗ ∗

10. Determine the result of the editing in the examples below:

a) 1 2 2 7   9 9 9 . 9 9 +   g) 1 9 7 $\overline{4}$ + + + . + + +

b) 2 1 0 0 0 $\overline{0}$ 9 9 9 D B P (4)   h) 0 0 7 5 $\overline{}$ − − − . − − − −

c) 0 0 1 2   V Z Z Z +   i) 1 9 3 3 $ $ $ $. $ $ +

d) 0 0 7 $\overline{5}$ − Z Z . Z Z Z Z   j) 9 6 $ $ $ $. $ $ C R

e) 0   P P P Z Z Z −   k) 8 $\overline{6}$ $ − − − . − −

f) 1 0 6 1   − $ ∗ ∗ V ∗ ∗   l) 0 $ − − − . − −

11. In the exercises a), b), c), and d) below data and corresponding edited results are given. Find a suitable picture for each exercise.

a) 0 1 7 3 0 0 2 4 $ ∗ 1 7 , 3 0 0 . 2 4

    0 0 0 0 0 1 7 $\overline{5}$ $ ∗ ∗ ∗ ∗ ∗ 1 . 7 5 C R

    0 0 0 0 0 0 0   ∗ ∗ ∗ ∗ ∗ ∗ ∗ ∗ . ∗ ∗ ∗ ∗

b) 3 7 1 1 0 6 3 5 7   3 7 1 1 0 6 , 3 5 7

    0   0 0 0 0 0 0 , 0 0 0

c) 0 0 0 0 0 1 2 $\overline{5}$ − 1 . 2 5

    1 2 3 1 4 6 8 1   1 2 3 , 1 4 6 . 8 1

    0   . 0 0

d) 0 0 0 1 2 7 8 0   1 2 7 . 8 0 +

    1 0 7 6 5 8 7 $\overline{2}$ 1 0 7 , 6 5 8 . 7 2 −

    0   0 0 0 . 0 0 +

12. Consider the two record descriptions:

```
0 1    A .
       0 2   B   P I C T U R E   X ( 6 ) .
       0 2   C   P I C T U R E   X ( 6 ) .
0 1    D .
       0 2   E   P I C T U R E   X ( 8 ) .
       0 2   F .
              0 3   G   P I C T U R E   X ( 8 )   J U S T I F I E D   R I G H T .
```

What will be the contents of D when the following sentences have been performed if B contains BAINES and C contains CHERRY.

a) MOVE B TO E MOVE C TO G.
b) MOVE A TO D.
c) MOVE B TO E MOVE C TO F.

13. Construct a complete record description for the record SALARY – SPECIFICATION of exercise 1 when the elementary items are characterized through:

EMP – NO	Positive integer with 4 digits.
NAME	20 alphabetic characters.
ADDR	20 alphanumeric characters.
PREL – TAX	Edited positive integer with 5 digits: at most 4 leading zeros are replaced by blanks, and the last 3 digits are separated from the preceding ones by a comma.
GROSS – PAY	Edited positive number with 7 digits, 2 of which are decimals: decimal point is inserted, leading integer zeros are replaced by blanks, and a comma is inserted before the last three integer digits.
SALARY	Edited positive number with 6 digits, 2 of which are decimals; edited as GROSS – PAY.
FEE	As SALARY.
VARIOUS IN EMOLUMENTS	Edited number with 6 digits, 2 of which are decimals: negative values are marked with CR, otherwise edited as GROSS – PAY.
PREL	Edited 4-digit integer: negative values marked with CR; at most 3 leading zeros are replaced by blanks, and the last 3 digits are separated from the preceding one by a comma.
ARREARS	As PREL.
VARIOUS IN DEDUCTIONS	As VARIOUS IN EMOLUMENTS.

NET – PAY   Edited number with 6 digits, 2 of which are decimals: negative values are marked with CR, leading integer zeros are replaced by asterisks, a comma is inserted between the first and the second digit, and the currency symbol is inserted.

14. a) Make a file description for a file with the name SUPPLIES whose records are not to be blocked and with standard label records where the file identification ID has the value "SUPPLIES". The file should contain one type of record with the name ARTICLE.

    b) Make a file description for a file with the name EMPLOYEES with 20 records in each block, no label records, and three record types with the names HOUR – EMP, WEEK – EMP, MONTH – EMP.

15. Which of the following entries are correct?

    a)   77   AA PICTURE 99V9 VALUE 14.15.
    b)   77   AA PICTURE 99V9 VALUE 14.
    c)   77   AA PICTURE 99V9 VALUE 14.1.
    d)   77   BB PICTURE 99.9 VALUE 14.1.
    e)   77   CC PICTURE X(5) VALUE "PI".
    f)   77   CC PICTURE X(5) VALUE "OMEGA".
    g)   77   CC PICTURE X(5) VALUE "EPSILON".

16. A table SALARY – TABLE has two entries, viz. 32 different salary classes and 3 different zones. Make a description of the table where the salary classes are groups called S – CLASS, each containing three 4-digit integer amounts called AMOUNT. How is a salary identified according to salary class 11 and zone 3?

Chapter 7. The environment division and the identification division

Chambers' caskets are just fine,
Made of sandalwood and pine.
If your loved ones have to go,
call Columbus 690.
If your loved ones pass away,
have them pass the Chambers way.
Chambers' customers all sing
"Death, o death, where is thy sting?"

TV COMMERCIAL FOR FUNERAL HOME

7.1. The environment division

ere we shall describe the environment division which constitutes the second division of a COBOL program. In this part the programmer associates problem-oriented concepts with the computer hardware which will actually run his program. The environment division begins with the heading ENVIRONMENT DIVISION and consists of two sections, the configuration section and the input-output section. Each of these sections has a number of fixed paragraphs as outlined below.

ENVIRONMENT DIVISION.
CONFIGURATION SECTION.
SOURCE – COMPUTER. contents-1
OBJECT – COMPUTER. contents-2
[SPECIAL – NAMES. contents-3]
[INPUT – OUTPUT SECTION.
FILE – CONTROL. contents-4
[I – O – CONTROL. contents-5]]

The *configuration section* contains a short description of the hardware equipment which will be used, and further designates certain units to be associated with problem-oriented concepts in the program. The first two paragraphs usually have the following simple formats:

SOURCE – COMPUTER. computer-name-1.
OBJECT – COMPUTER. computer-name-2.

Computer-name-1 and computer-name-2 stand for the names of the computers to be used for compiling and for execution; most often this is done on the same computer. Normally the paragraphs have only an identifying function. However, the formats may be enlarged to include clauses which state that only certain parts of the computer will be used for the processing or which connect units normally having another function with the machine. These options are highly machine dependent and the programmer should consult the COBOL manual for his computer for the exact specifications and options.

In the paragraph SPECIAL – NAMES implementor-names are associated with mnemonic names according to certain formats. The simplest of these is the following:

implementor-name IS mnemonic-name

Suppose that the environment division has the following paragraph:

SPECIAL-NAMES. TAPE-READER IS RANDOM-SEQUENCE.

In several places in the procedure division we may have the statement ACCEPT RANDOM – NUMBER FROM RANDOM – SEQUENCE with the result that a number is read from the tape-reader which provides a sequence of random numbers. If for some reason the program must be transferred to another computer with other input facilities, it suffices to replace the word TAPE – READER in the SPECIAL – NAMES-paragraph with some other name for a suitable input unit. There is another longer format which may be used when the console has switches whose positions can be tested in the program:

implementor-name [IS mnemonic-name]

$$\begin{cases} \text{ON STATUS IS condition-name-1 [OFF STATUS IS condition-name-2]} \\ \text{OFF STATUS IS condition-name-3 [ON STATUS IS condition-name-4]} \end{cases}$$

The implementor-name must be the name of a switch. The condition-names here correspond to a special kind of conditional variables, viz. positions of a switch. Their hardware connection makes it necessary that they be specified in the environment division and not in the data division. Example:

SPECIAL-NAMES.
    SWITCH-4 ON STATUS IS CONTROL-PRINT-OUT.

CONTROL – PRINT – OUT is then a condition-name which can enter the procedure division in the same way as an ordinary condition in an IF- or PERFORM-statement. In the statement IF CONTROL – PRINT – OUT DISPLAY ACT – NUMBER the status of SWITCH – 4 on the console is tested; if it is ON the DISPLAY-statement is executed. The SPECIAL – NAMES-paragraph may contain several clauses one after the other.

In the *input-output section* the two paragraphs headed by FILE – CONTROL and I – O – CONTROL are used for connecting the files to

96

external storage media, and for devising some special control techniques related to input or output. For the FILE – CONTROL- paragraph the following format is usually sufficient:

FILE – CONTROL.

$$\{ \underline{\text{SELECT}} \; [\underline{\text{OPTIONAL}}] \; \text{file-name-1} \; [\underline{\text{RENAMING}} \; \text{file-name-2}]$$

$$\underline{\text{ASSIGN}} \; \text{TO} \; \text{implementor-name-1} \; [, \text{implementor-name-2}] \ldots$$

$$[\text{FOR} \; \underline{\text{MULTIPLE}} \; \underline{\text{REEL}}]$$

$$\left[, \underline{\text{RESERVE}} \left\{ \begin{array}{c} \text{integer} \\ \underline{\text{NO}} \end{array} \right\} \text{ALTERNATE} \left[\begin{array}{c} \text{AREA} \\ \text{AREAS} \end{array} \right] \right] . \} \ldots$$

SELECT file-name ASSIGN implementor-names is the nucleus in the format which determines to which external units a file is assigned. The following example shows how the file STOCK is assigned to the external unit TAPE – UNIT – 1, and UPDATE – FILE is assigned to TAPE – UNIT – 2 and TAPE – UNIT – 3:

```
F I L E - C O N T R O L .   S E L E C T   S T O C K   A S S I G N   T O   T A P E - U N I T - 1 .
        S E L E C T   U P D A T E - F I L E   A S S I G N   T O   T A P E - U N I T - 2
        A N D   T A P E - U N I T - 3 .
```

It is evident from the format that there are several alternatives possible when assigning files to external units. The word OPTIONAL is used to show that the file may be empty, i.e. it may be completely devoid of data. This might be the case for a file which contains changes regarding a master file for a certain time period if no changes have occurred during that period. When OPTIONAL has been specified the machine stops when the file is opened, and the operator is then via the console supposed to tell the computer whether the file contains data or not. If it is empty, then on the first READ which concerns this file the AT END-phrase is executed, and the standard end-of-file processing is not performed for this file.

When a file has exactly the same structure as another file we can add the clause RENAMING file-name-2 directly after the file-name. In this way the file description (including the record descriptions) of file-name-2 will become valid also for the first file, and of course it must not have a separate file description in the data division. Otherwise, the files are independent, associated with different external units and with different areas reserved in the internal storage. In the procedure division data-names on all lower levels must be qualified by the file-names.

A long file stored on magnetic tape sometimes needs several reels. One solution of this problem is to assign the file to the same number of tape units as the number of reels. However, since the reels are read or written one at a time in succession, several tape units will unnecessarily be standing by during processing. By using the MULTIPLE REEL-clause the programmer is able to make the tape units operate on several sets of reels. The procedure for exchange of reels is specified in the COBOL system manual for the computer used.

Some computers are built in such a way that transfers between external units and the internal storage can be performed while the central processor is working with another part of the storage. This process is called data buffering. For instance, buffering can be applied in transferring new records from an external unit to the internal storage at the same time as the preceding records of the file are processed in another storage area. In this way much time can be saved. Every COBOL system has, in this respect, a standard buffering technique which, however, can be modified by an option of the RESERVE-clause. For the exact effect of the RESERVE-clause the programmer must see the system manual for his computer.

The paragraph I – O – CONTROL has essentially the following format:

I – O – CONTROL.

[APPLY input-output-technique ON file-name-1 [, file-name-2]...]...

$$[; \underline{RERUN} \left[\underline{ON} \left\{ \begin{array}{l} \text{file-name-3} \\ \underline{\text{implementor-name}} \end{array} \right\} \right]$$

$$EVERY \left\{ \begin{array}{l} \underline{END \ OF \ REEL} \\ \text{integer } \underline{RECORDS} \end{array} \right\} OF \ \text{file-name-4]} ...$$

[; SAME [RECORD] AREA FOR file-name-5 {, file-name-6} ...]... .

The word APPLY indicates that some special technique should be used on input or output, but for closer details we must defer to the system manuals. After the word RERUN we can state when we want memory dumps to be performed in order to simplify a restart if a machine error would occur. With the clause SAME RECORD AREA we introduce the possibility of letting records of different files share internal storage area. This would be handy e.g. if a record which has just been read in is only updated to be written out again. No transfer in the internal storage will then be necessary. With SAME AREA only, the files will also share all buffer areas; in this case no two of the files can be open simultaneously.

Finally we give an example of a complete environment division:

```
ENVIRONMENT DIVISION.
CONFIGURATION SECTION.
SOURCE-COMPUTER. COMPONE.
OBJECT-COMPUTER. COMPTWO.
SPECIAL-NAMES. UNIT-1 IS OUTPUT-DATA
     SWITCH-2 ON IS SPECIAL-MEASURES
     OFF IS NORMAL-TREATMENT.
INPUT-OUTPUT SECTION.
FILE-CONTROL. SELECT STOCK-IN ASSIGN TAPE-UNIT-1
     AND TAPE-UNIT-2 FOR MULTIPLE REEL.
     SELECT STOCK-OUT RENAMING STOCK-IN ASSIGN
     TAPE-UNIT-3 AND TAPE-UNIT-4 FOR MULTIPLE REEL.
     SELECT OPTIONAL CHANGES ASSIGN TO CARD-READER.
     SELECT ORDERS ASSIGN TO PRINTER.
```

I-O-CONTROL. RERUN ON TAPE-UNIT-5 EVERY 1000
RECORDS OF STOCK-IN SAME RECORD AREA FOR
STOCK-IN, STOCK-OUT.

This environment division fulfils the following assumptions. The program
will be compiled on the computer COMPONE and run on COMPTWO. The
external unit UNIT-1 will be used in some special connection, e.g. as the
output device in a DISPLAY-statement, and is identified in the procedure
division by the mnemonic name OUTPUT-DATA. The positions of
SWITCH-2 are assumed to determine a condition during the processing.
In the program four files will be treated. The files STOCK-IN and
STOCK-OUT are stored on an arbitrary number of tape reels, and for
each file the tapes are treated alternately on two tape units. The two files
have an identical description, and only STOCK-IN has to be described in
the data division. The file CHANGES can be empty. For every 1000 records
in STOCK-IN a memory dump will be performed on TAPE-UNIT-5.
The same internal storage area is used for records in STOCK-IN and
STOCK-OUT.

7.2. The identification division

The first division of the COBOL program, the identification division, is a
label of the program with certain information collected in paragraphs with
fixed names. The identification division does not affect the activity of the
computer but serves merely as an identification of source program and
object program, especially on print-outs during compilation. The paragraphs must appear in the following order:

IDENTIFICATION DIVISION.
PROGRAM-ID. program-name.
[AUTHOR. comment]
[INSTALLATION. comment]
[DATE-WRITTEN. comment]
[DATE-COMPILED. comment]
[SECURITY. comment]
[REMARKS. comment]

The paragraph PROGRAM-ID is the only compulsory paragraph. The
program-name must obey the same rules as are valid for the formation of
words. For the paragraph DATE-COMPILED it should be noted that
regardless of the contents, the comment will be replaced by the current
date on output listing of the source program during compilation. All
comments may consist of arbitrary sequences of COBOL characters and

must be terminated by a period followed by space. Note that the identification of a new paragraph assumes that its name begins at the A-margin.

Example:

```
IDENTIFICATION DIVISION.
PROGRAM-ID.  UPDATING-OF-REGISTERS.
AUTHOR.  N.N.
INSTALLATION.  CIA.
DATE-WRITTEN.  67-11-15.
DATE-COMPILED.  TO-DAY.
SECURITY.  RED-TAPE.
```

Exercise

1. Write an environment division containing the following information:
   a) Compilation as well as running should be performed on the computer AJAX.
   b) The files F–FILE, TRANSACTIONS, and G–FILE should be assigned to the external units TAPE–UNIT–4, CARD–READER, and PRINTER. The file F–FILE may need several reels while TRANSACTIONS may be empty.
   c) Memory dump should be performed on DRUM each time one reel of F–FILE has been processed.

Chapter 8. Some simple COBOL programs

8.1. Inventory control

Maintenance of inventory records is a frequent use of computers in business. Most often, the inventory is comprised of many different kinds of goods which are delivered to different customers at a varying rate. Before a certain item in the stock is depleted it must be reordered from a supplier. The reorders each require some time before delivery because of shipping time and availability at the supplier's factory. Many inventory control systems are based on a reorder point, i.e. a reorder is made when stock on hand drops to a set reorder level. The reorder point and an adequate reorder quantity are determined by an analysis of the variations in customer demand and the delivery times from suppliers. The risk of being caught short of an item must be weighed against the extra cost of keeping a larger inventory on hand.

In the following program we will give an example that shows how inventory records on a stock of goods can be maintained by a computer. The master inventory file is to be updated daily by recording the transactions that have taken place in the stock during the day. The master inventory file should contain current values of quantities in stock, ordered quantities, and accumulated consumption during the year. A list of the items to be reordered should be printed each day. In order to produce a reorder list we must store reorder points and reorder quantities for each item in the master file. In this program example we confine ourselves to three types of transactions: the receipt of ordered goods, reordering, and delivery of goods. More drastic changes of the files such as insertion of new or deletion of old items, or changes in identifiers and in principles of reordering, are taken care of by other programs.

The daily transactions are punched on cards and form a file of daily records. A code consisting of a single digit indicates the type of transaction;

the digit 1 for a receipt, 2 for a reorder, and 3 for a customer delivery. Several transactions may occur on the same day for an item in inventory. The master file and the transaction file are assumed to be sorted on an item number. The transaction file is also sorted by the chronological order in which the transactions occur so that no partial summations will give absurd values.

```
IDENTIFICATION DIVISION.
PROGRAM-ID. INVENTORY-CONTROL.
AUTHOR. A.L-D.

ENVIRONMENT DIVISION.
CONFIGURATION SECTION.
SOURCE-COMPUTER. AJAX.
OBJECT-COMPUTER. AJAX.
INPUT-OUTPUT SECTION.
FILE-CONTROL. SELECT OLD-MASTER ASSIGN TO TAPE-1.
     SELECT NEW-MASTER ASSIGN TO TAPE-3.
     SELECT TRANSACTION ASSIGN TO CARD-READER.
     SELECT ORDER-LIST ASSIGN TO PRINTER.

DATA DIVISION.
FILE SECTION.
FD   OLD-MASTER LABEL RECORDS OMITTED;
     DATA RECORD IS OLD.
01   OLD.
     02 ITEM-NO PICTURE 9(6).
     02 NAME PICTURE X(24).
     02 MEASURE PICTURE X(4).
     02 R-POINT PICTURE 9(6).
     02 R-QUANT PICTURE 9(6).
     02 Q-IN-STOCK PICTURE 9(6).
     02 Q-ON-ORDER PICTURE 9(6).
     02 TOT-CONS PICTURE 9(8).
FD   NEW-MASTER LABEL RECORDS OMITTED;
     DATA RECORD IS NEW.
01   NEW.
     02 ITEM-NO PICTURE 9(6).
     02 NAME PICTURE X(24).
     02 MEASURE PICTURE X(4).
     02 R-POINT PICTURE 9(6).
     02 R-QUANT PICTURE 9(6).
     02 Q-IN-STOCK PICTURE 9(6).
     02 Q-ON-ORDER PICTURE 9(6).
     02 TOT-CONS PICTURE 9(8).
FD   TRANSACTION LABEL RECORDS OMITTED;
     DATA RECORD IS TR.
01   TR.
     02 ITEM-NO PICTURE 9(6).
     02 OCC-NO PICTURE 99.
     02 CODE-NO PICTURE 9.
     02 Q PICTURE 9(6).
FD   ORDER-LIST LABEL RECORDS OMITTED;
     DATA RECORD IS ORDER.
01   ORDER.
     02 ITEM-NO PICTURE 9(6).
     02 NAME PICTURE BBX(24).
     02 R-QUANT PICTURE Z(8).
     02 MEASURE PICTURE BBX(4).
CONSTANT SECTION.
77   MAX-NO PICTURE 9(6) VALUE IS 999999.
```

```
PROCEDURE DIVISION.
START.  OPEN INPUT OLD-MASTER, TRANSACTION
    OUTPUT NEW-MASTER, ORDER-LIST.
RTR.  READ TRANSACTION AT END MOVE MAX-NO TO
    ITEM-NO IN TR.
NEW-OLD.  READ OLD-MASTER AT END
    DISPLAY "UPDATING READY" GO TO FINIS.
    IF ITEM-NO IN OLD LESS ITEM-NO IN TR
    GO TO NEW-NEW.
EQUALITY.  GO TO RECEIPT, REORDER, DELIVERY
    DEPENDING ON CODE-NO.
RECEIPT.  ADD Q TO Q-IN-STOCK IN OLD.
    SUBTRACT Q FROM Q-ON-ORDER IN OLD.
    GO TO NEW-TR.
REORDER.  ADD Q TO Q-ON-ORDER IN OLD.  GO TO NEW-TR.
DELIVERY.  SUBTRACT Q FROM Q-IN-STOCK IN OLD.
    ADD Q TO TOT-CONS IN OLD.
NEW-TR.  PERFORM RTR.
    IF ITEM-NO IN OLD EQUAL TO ITEM-NO IN TR
    GO TO EQUALITY.
    IF Q-IN-STOCK IN OLD + Q-ON-ORDER IN OLD
    LESS R-POINT IN OLD MOVE ITEM-NO IN OLD TO
    ITEM-NO IN ORDER MOVE NAME IN OLD TO NAME IN
    ORDER MOVE R-QUANT IN OLD TO R-QUANT IN ORDER
    MOVE MEASURE IN OLD TO MEASURE IN ORDER
    WRITE ORDER.
NEW-NEW.  WRITE NEW FROM OLD.  GO TO NEW-OLD.
FINIS.  CLOSE OLD-MASTER, TRANSACTION,
    NEW-MASTER, ORDER-LIST.  STOP RUN.
```

The program starts with the identification division which contains the name of the program and the name of the author. In the environment division the four files are assigned to hardware units; the master file which is to be processed is given the name OLD–MASTER and the updated master file is called NEW–MASTER. These files are assigned to one tape unit each. The transactions form the file TRANSACTION on punched cards, and the ORDER–LIST is to be produced on a printer.

In the data division the files are described under the header FILE SECTION. OLD–MASTER and NEW–MASTER contain the records OLD and NEW, respectively, with identical structures. These records have as identifiers the item number ITEM–NO, the name NAME, and the unit of measure MEASURE which is used in reordering. The reorder point R–POINT and the reorder quantity R–QUANT are not changed by this program. The quantity in stock Q–IN–STOCK, the quantity on order but not yet received Q–ON–ORDER, and the accumulated year-to-date consumption TOT–CONS are controlled by the program. The record TR in TRANSACTION contains the item number, the occurrence number OCC–NO which is not used in this program but in an earlier sorting of the transaction file, the code digit CODE–NO, and the current quantity Q. The record ORDER in ORDER–LIST corresponds to the print-out of the quantity of a certain item to be reordered, this item being described by number, name, and unit of measure. It should be observed that the picture of the elementary items to be printed out contain editing symbols. In the constant section the elementary item MAX – NO obtains a value which is greater than all item numbers. MAX – NO is used in the procedure division as the item number of a fictitious record which is assumed to terminate the file TRANSACTION. By this arrangement the procedure division can be simplified since the same kind of comparison of the item numbers in the files OLD – MASTER and TRANSACTION can be made during the whole run even when there are no more records in TRANSACTION to be read.

In the first paragraph of the procedure division, START, all the files are opened. In the paragraph RTR a record is read from the transaction file. This sentence will be performed several times during the run and when all the records have been read, the value of MAX – NO is assigned to ITEM – NO in TR. In NEW – OLD a record is read from OLD – MASTER. This sentence is also repeated several times, and when all the records have been read a print-out is obtained indicating that the updating is completed and the program control is transferred to the paragraph FINIS. In this paragraph the files are closed and the run of the program is terminated. If after reading a record from OLD – MASTER it is found that the item number in OLD is less than the item number in TR, this means that no transaction has occurred for the current item number in OLD and the contents of OLD are moved directly to the file NEW – MASTER. After that a GO-statement leads back to the paragraph NEW – OLD and the next record in OLD – MASTER is processed. If the item numbers agree a jump takes place in the paragraph EQUALITY to one of the paragraphs RECEIPT, REORDER, or DELIVERY and there the record OLD is updated in different ways; the destination of the jump depends on the code digit in TR. Then the transaction records are read one by one, and as long as the item number agrees with that in OLD, a GO-statement will lead to the paragraph EQUALITY, and the record OLD is updated anew. When a new item number appears in TR the updating of OLD is completed and a test is made whether the sum of Q – IN – STOCK and Q – ON – ORDER is less than the value of R – POINT. If this is the case the record ORDER is formed and written out on printer. In any case the record OLD is finally moved to NEW – MASTER. Then there is a jump to NEW – OLD and the next record in OLD – MASTER is treated in the same way as the preceding one.

8.2. Indexing of newspaper articles

We shall now give an example of a program which indicates the usefulness of COBOL in documentation problems. A body of newspaper articles is recorded. Every article has been registered by the title and an identification number specifying where to find the article in the archives. Certain words in the titles that particularly characterize the contents of the articles are preceded by an asterisk and are considered as key words. Each word is supposed to end with a space. The titles together with the identification numbers are assumed to be stored on an input file which can be processed by a computer.

Every title is now to be scanned systematically, and for every discovered key word a new record should be formed with the key word stored in a fixed place of the record. Furthermore, this new record shall contain the title with all the asterisks removed, and the identification number. These records will then form an output file, and it is the aim of our COBOL program to create this file. After that, the output file, if stored on a convenient medium, may be sorted with respect to the key words by means of a standard sort program; such standard programs are available at most installations. The problem described here may, of course, be generalized to the search for any other individual character or string of characters, but we have found it convenient to restrict the problem to the search for just an asterisk.

The length of the titles has been fixed to 150 characters, unused character positions being filled by spaces. The identification number consists of 6 digits. For the key word of the new record 24 character positions are reserved; longer key words will be truncated.

```
IDENTIFICATION DIVISION.
PROGRAM-ID. INDEXING-OF-ARTICLES.
AUTHOR. ANNA LYSEGARD.

ENVIRONMENT DIVISION.
CONFIGURATION SECTION.
SOURCE-COMPUTER. AJAX.
OBJECT-COMPUTER. AJAX.
INPUT-OUTPUT SECTION.
FILE-CONTROL. SELECT INPUT-FILE ASSIGN TO UNIT-1.
     SELECT OUTPUT-FILE ASSIGN TO UNIT-4.
DATA DIVISION.
FILE SECTION.
FD   INPUT-FILE
     LABEL RECORDS OMITTED
     DATA RECORD IS ARTICLE.
01   ARTICLE.
     02 TITLE PICTURE X OCCURS 150.
     02 IDT PICTURE 9(6).
FD   OUTPUT-FILE
     LABEL RECORDS OMITTED
     DATA RECORD IS SORT-RECORD.
01   SORT-RECORD.
     02 KEY-WORD.
          03 KWCHAR PICTURE X OCCURS 24.
     02 TITLE-S PICTURE X OCCURS 150.
     02 IDT-S PICTURE 9(6).
WORKING-STORAGE SECTION.
77   I PICTURE 999 COMPUTATIONAL.
77   J PICTURE 999 COMPUTATIONAL.
77   K PICTURE 999 COMPUTATIONAL.
77   T PICTURE X.
```

```
PROCEDURE DIVISION.
START. OPEN INPUT INPUT-FILE OUTPUT OUTPUT-FILE.
READ-INPUT-FILE. READ INPUT-FILE AT END
       GO TO FINIS. MOVE 1 TO K.
KEY-WORD-TEST. IF TITLE (K) EQUAL TO "*" GO TO
       STORE-KEY-WORD.
K2. ADD 1 TO K IF K GREATER 150 GO TO
       READ-INPUT-FILE. GO TO KEY-WORD-TEST.
STORE-KEY-WORD. MOVE SPACES TO KEY-WORD
       MOVE 1 TO J.
SK2. ADD 1 TO K
       IF K NOT GREATER 150 MOVE TITLE (K) TO T
       IF T NOT EQUAL TO SPACE MOVE T TO KWCHAR (J)
       IF J LESS 24 ADD 1 TO J GO TO SK2.
MOVE-TITLE. MOVE 1 TO I, J.
MT2. MOVE TITLE (I) TO T
       IF T EQUAL TO "*" GO TO MT3.
       MOVE T TO TITLE-S (J) ADD 1 TO J.
       IF I EQUAL TO 150 GO TO MT4.
MT3. ADD 1 TO I GO TO MT2.
MT4. IF J GREATER 150 GO TO WRITE-SORT-RECORD.
       MOVE SPACE TO TITLE-S (J) ADD 1 TO J
       GO TO MT4.
WRITE-SORT-RECORD. MOVE IDT TO IDT-S
       WRITE SORT-RECORD GO TO K2.
FINIS. CLOSE INPUT-FILE, OUTPUT-FILE
       DISPLAY "OUTPUT-FILE IS COMPLETED" STOP RUN.
```

The identification division and the environment division hardly need any explanation. In the data division two files are defined, INPUT–FILE and OUTPUT–FILE, with one type of record each, ARTICLE and SORT–RECORD, respectively. The record descriptions correspond to the conditions regarding the contents of the records. A title must be interpreted as a table of single characters, since we want to perform tests on these characters. In the procedure division the key word in SORT–RECORD is considered in one case as a unit, in another as a table of characters, and therefore it has been described as a group of elementary items which at the same time constitutes a table. In the working-storage section we describe three integers I, J, K which serve as tallies in the scanning and moving of tables. T is an auxiliary variable which is easier to deal with than the subscripted variables used in the program.

In the procedure division the files are opened in the paragraph START. Every record is read in the paragraph READ–INPUT–FILE and processed in the rest of the program. When all the records have been treated the paragraph FINIS is performed and after that the computer is ready to execute another program. The processing of a record starts by examining the characters of the title, one by one, until an asterisk is discovered. This search uses the variable K as a tally. If an asterisk appears, the control is transferred to the paragraph STORE–KEY–WORD. When the last character of the title has been examined, a new record is read and processed in the same way. The storing of the key words is initiated by filling the character positions reserved for KEY–WORD with spaces, i.e. all previous information is erased. Then all the characters, maximized at 24, after the asterisk are moved to the storage area of KEY – WORD until a space appears, and K is increased accordingly. When the key word has been moved, i.e. when some condition in the paragraph SK2 is not satisfied, the control is transferred to the paragraph MOVE – TITLE, and TITLE is moved to TITLE – S of SORT – RECORD. All asterisks are removed and TITLE – S is compressed. Finally IDT is moved to IDT – S, SORT – RECORD is written on OUTPUT – FILE, and a jump is made to the paragraph K2, where the searching for another key word in the same title begins.

8.3. Census

We are now going to discuss a simplified example of census. We assume a certain geographic area which is small enough that the number of children born on any given day will never exceed 999. Further we assume that no person is more than 99 years old. Hence, to identify a person it suffices to give his date of birth together with a 3-digit identification number which we assume is odd for men, even for women. For example, John Doe who was the second male born on December 4, 1934, may be identified as 341204003. All initial data are stored in a master file on magnetic tape. We will call the file OLD and suppose that it contains records with the following items: a) year of birth, 2 digits; b) month of birth, 2 digits; c) day of birth, 2 digits; d) birth number, 3 digits; e) name, 60 characters; f) address, 60 characters; g) civil status, 1 letter.

A file called TRANSACTION contains three types of transactions codified according to the rules: $0 =$ birth or moving in; $1 =$ change in name, address, or civil status; $2 =$ death or moving out. For every person in this file a code digit and current information of all the items present in the records on the master file are to be punched on cards. Since every card can accomodate at most 80 characters and each individual requires 131 characters, two punched card records per individual are used. Only one transaction may occur per person. In both files the records are ordered in ascending sequence on the nine digits in the elementary items a) through d). Our task is to produce an updated master file NEW with the same structure as OLD. The code digit 0 in the transactions shall cause the registration of a new person on the master file, the code digit 1 the replacement of old values by new, and code digit 2 the elimination of a person from the master file. (In the last case all data not having an identifying function may be replaced by spaces.)

Further the number of people aged 6 and 66 and the number of men and women are to be computed for the file NEW. In addition, for every person aged 6 we want to have a special form printed (to be used on registration in school) with the name at the top of the page, address two lines below, and the identification number three lines further below. The current year is read from a standard input unit by an ACCEPT-statement.

```
IDENTIFICATION DIVISION.
PROGRAM-ID. CENSUS.
AUTHOR. ANNA LYSEGARD.
DATE-WRITTEN. 1 SEPTEMBER 1967.
DATE-COMPILED. TO-DAY.

ENVIRONMENT DIVISION.
CONFIGURATION SECTION.
SOURCE-COMPUTER. COMPONE.
OBJECT-COMPUTER. COMPTWO.
SPECIAL-NAMES. TOP-OF-FORM IS NEW-PAPER.
INPUT-OUTPUT SECTION.
FILE-CONTROL. SELECT OLD ASSIGN TO TAPE-1.
     SELECT NEW ASSIGN TO TAPE-2.
     SELECT TRANSACTION ASSIGN TO CARD-READER.
     SELECT PAPERS ASSIGN TO PRINTER.

DATA DIVISION.
FILE SECTION.
FD   OLD BLOCK CONTAINS 50 RECORDS LABEL RECORDS
     ARE STANDARD DATA RECORD IS OP.
01   OP.
     02   ID-NUMBER.
          03 YEAR PICTURE IS 9(2).
          03 MONTH PICTURE IS 9(2).
          03 DAY PICTURE IS 9(2).
          03 NR PICTURE IS 9(3).
     02 NAME PICTURE IS X(60).
     02 ADDR PICTURE IS X(60).
     02 STAT PICTURE IS A.
FD   NEW BLOCK CONTAINS 50 RECORDS LABEL RECORDS
     ARE STANDARD DATA RECORD IS NP.
01   NP.
     02   ID-NUMBER.
          03 YEAR PICTURE IS 9(2).
          03 MONTH PICTURE IS 9(2).
          03 DAY PICTURE IS 9(2).
          03 NR PICTURE IS 9(3).
     02   NAME PICTURE IS X(60).
     02   ADDR PICTURE IS X(60).
     02   STAT PICTURE IS A.
FD   TRANSACTION LABEL RECORDS ARE OMITTED
     DATA RECORDS ARE TR-1, TR-2.
01   TR-1.
     02   ID-NUMBER PICTURE IS 9(9).
     02   NAME PICTURE IS X(60).
01   TR-2.
     02   ID-NUMBER PICTURE IS 9(9).
     02   ADDR PICTURE IS X(60).
     02   STAT PICTURE IS A.
     02   CODE-DIGIT PICTURE IS 9.
FD   PAPERS LABEL RECORDS ARE OMITTED
     DATA RECORDS ARE NAME, ADDR, ID-NUMBER.
01   NAME PICTURE IS X(60).
01   ADDR PICTURE IS X(60).
01   ID-NUMBER PICTURE IS 9(9).
WORKING-STORAGE SECTION.
77   MEN PICTURE IS 9(7) VALUE IS ZERO.
77   WOMEN PICTURE IS 9(7) VALUE IS ZERO.
77   SCHOOL PICTURE IS 9(6) VALUE IS ZERO.
```

```
77    PENSION PICTURE IS 9(6) VALUE IS ZERO.
77    A PICTURE IS 9(3).
77    B PICTURE IS 9.
77    C PICTURE IS 9(2).
77    D PICTURE IS 9(2).
77    THIS-YEAR PICTURE IS 9(2).
01    TR.
      02    ID-NUMBER PICTURE IS 9(9).
      02    NAME PICTURE IS X(60).
      02    ADDR PICTURE IS X(60).
      02    STAT PICTURE IS A.

PROCEDURE DIVISION.
BEGIN. OPEN INPUT OLD, TRANSACTION OUTPUT NEW,
      PAPERS. ACCEPT THIS-YEAR.
      IF THIS-YEAR > 5 COMPUTE C = THIS-YEAR - 6
      ELSE COMPUTE C = THIS-YEAR + 94.
      IF THIS-YEAR > 65 COMPUTE D = THIS-YEAR - 66
      ELSE COMPUTE D = THIS-YEAR + 34.
READ-OLD. READ OLD RECORD AT END GO TO OLD-FINIS.
READ-TR-1. READ TRANSACTION RECORD AT END GO TO
      TRANS-FINIS.
MOVE-TR-1. MOVE ID-NUMBER IN TR-1 TO ID-NUMBER IN
      TR. MOVE NAME IN TR-1 TO NAME IN TR.
READ-TR-2. READ TRANSACTION RECORD
      AT END DISPLAY "TRANSACTION NOT CORRECT"
      GO TO FINIS.
MOVE-TR-2. MOVE ADDR IN TR-2 TO ADDR IN TR.
      MOVE STAT IN TR-2 TO STAT IN TR.
COMPARE. IF ID-NUMBER IN OP < ID-NUMBER IN TR
      GO TO OLD-ONLY.
      IF CODE-DIGIT < 2 MOVE TR TO NP PERFORM COUNT.
      IF CODE-DIGIT = 0 GO TO READ-TR-1
      ELSE GO TO READ-OLD.
OLD-ONLY. MOVE OP TO NP. PERFORM COUNT.
      READ OLD RECORD AT END GO TO OLD-F-F.
      GO TO COMPARE.
OLD-FINIS. READ TRANSACTION RECORD
      AT END GO TO FINIS.
      PERFORM MOVE-TR-1.
      READ TRANSACTION RECORD AT END
      DISPLAY "TRANSACTION NOT CORRECT" GO TO FINIS.
      PERFORM MOVE-TR-2.
OLD-F-F. MOVE TR TO NP. PERFORM COUNT.
      GO TO OLD-FINIS.
TRANS-FINIS. MOVE OP TO NP. PERFORM COUNT. READ
      OLD AT END GO TO FINIS. GO TO TRANS-FINIS.
FINIS. DISPLAY MEN, SPACE, WOMEN, SPACE, SCHOOL,
      SPACE, PENSION.
      CLOSE OLD, NEW, TRANSACTION, PAPERS.
      STOP RUN.
COUNT. DIVIDE 2 INTO NR IN NP GIVING A.
      MULTIPLY 2 BY A.
      SUBTRACT A FROM NR IN NP GIVING B.
      IF B = 1 ADD 1 TO MEN ELSE ADD 1 TO WOMEN.
      IF YEAR IN NP = C ADD 1 TO SCHOOL
      WRITE NAME IN PAPERS FROM NAME IN NP
      AFTER ADVANCING NEW-PAPER
      WRITE ADDR IN PAPERS FROM ADDR IN NP
      AFTER ADVANCING 2 LINES
      WRITE ID-NUMBER IN PAPERS FROM ID-NUMBER IN NP
      AFTER ADVANCING 3 LINES.
      IF YEAR IN NP = D ADD 1 TO PENSION.
      WRITE NP.
```

In the environment division there is a SPECIAL – NAMES-paragraph where TOP – OF – FORM is an implementor-name which is used to get the printer to begin on a new page. In the data division a transaction is divided into two records TR – 1 and TR – 2. ID – NUMBER in TR – 2 is not used in the program but has been used in an earlier phase for a merging sort with the records ·rR – 1. The record TR in the working-storage section defines a memory space where the information from the records TR – 1 and TR – 2 is stored together. In the first paragraph of the procedure division the year of birth C for persons aged 6 and D for persons aged 66 are computed with two digits. The paragraph COUNT begins with an examination if the birth number is even or odd.

Exercises

1. It is assumed that a sequence of records containing data of employees in a company are stored on a file on magnetic tape. Every record contains:

    a) employee number (4 digits)
    b) name (40 characters)
    c) address (40 characters)
    d) information on ordinary salary (4 digits)
    e) accumulated salary (5 digits)

    The file is sorted on employee number and has no labels. At the end of every month it will be matched against a transaction file on punched cards, in which every individual in the master file may occur at most once. A transaction indicates an occasional change of the salary as specified by a code. If the code digit is greater than 49 the change means a salary increment, otherwise a deduction. Every record of the transaction file contains:

    a) employee number (4 digits)
    b) code (2 digits)
    c) amount (4 digits)

    Write a COBOL program which will produce an updated master file, where the accumulated salary has been increased by the current salary. For every employee a notice should be printed containing the following information:

    At the top of the notice: name
    2 lines below: address
    4 lines further below: ordinary salary, change (with leading plus or minus sign), actual salary, accumulated salary.

The program is to be compiled and run on the well-known computer AJAX with the tape units TAPE – UNIT – 1 and TAPE – UNIT – 2, the card reader CARD – READER, and the printer PRINTER. The printer is directed to a new page by the implementor-name TOP – OF – FORM.

2. On behalf of the electricity works a program is to be prepared for the production of accounts to subscribers in connection with the collection of charges. The charge is composed of a subscription fee depending on the subscription class to which the subscriber belongs, and a consumption charge which is the product of the rate and the number of kWh used. The latter is computed as the difference between the present and the previous meter positions.

The programmer has at his disposal a master file, stored on magnetic tape, containing information on the subscribers, one record for each subscriber. Every record contains:

a) subscription number (6 digits)
b) subscriber's name (40 characters)
c) subscriber's address (40 characters)
d) subscription class (2 computational digits with values from 1 to 10)
e) previous meter position (6 digits)
f) year-to-date consumption (5 computational digits)

The records are ordered on ascending subscription numbers and blocked together with 100 records in each block. The file has standard labels and is to be matched against a transaction file on punched cards, whose records contain a subscription number (6 digits) and the present meter position (6 digits). The transaction file is supposed to be sorted on ascending subscription numbers and every subscriber of the master file may occur not more than once.

Write a COBOL program updating the master file and printing for every subscriber in the transaction file an account containing:

At the top of the account: subscription number, name, address, subscription class,
4 lines below: previous meter position, present meter position, subscription fee, consumption charge, total amount to pay.

The subscription fee has three integer positions and the last two quantities five. They have all two decimals and floating insertion of currency symbol up to the last integer position is required.

The master file is updated by replacing the previous meter position by the present and adding the number of kWh used to the year-to-date consumption. If a subscriber does not occur on the transaction file the corresponding record of the master file is written unchanged on the new master file.

The rate (2 computational decimals) and a tariff consisting of the ten subscription fees, one for each subscription class, (each fee consisting of 3 computational digits) are accepted from a standard unit before the processing of the files starts. For each ACCEPT-statement one elementary item is accepted.

The program is to be compiled and run on the powerful computer ZEUS with the tape units TAPE – 1, TAPE – 2, a printer PRINTER, and a card reader CARD – READER. The implementor-name used to get the printer to start on a new account form is TOP – OF – FORM. It may be assumed that subscription numbers are less than 999999. The case when the meter has made a complete turn so that the present meter position has a lower value than the previous one must also be considered.

Chapter 9. Further options in COBOL

Ainsi l'avait établi Gargantua. En leur règle n'était que cette clause: Fais ce que voudras.

FRANÇOIS RABELAIS

9.1. Introduction

reviously we have described the COBOL features used to write programs for the processing of sequential files. In this chapter we are going to describe additional, more powerful, possibilities which can be used in the procedure division and the data division. Also, we treat the usage of the COBOL library and segmentation. Further, the complete COBOL contains elements designed for use of random access storages, where data records may be processed non-sequentially, for sorting, and for report writing. The last three sections of the chapter will give a brief review on these subjects.

9.2. The procedure division

When we want to move, add, or subtract several elementary items by one single verb, MOVE, ADD, or SUBTRACT, we may use the COBOL word CORRESPONDING. The formats are:

MOVE CORRESPONDING identifier-1 TO identifier-2

ADD CORRESPONDING identifier-1 TO identifier-2 [ROUNDED]
    [; ON SIZE ERROR imperative-statement]

SUBTRACT CORRESPONDING identifier-1
    FROM identifier-2 [ROUNDED]
    [; ON SIZE ERROR imperative-statement]

If, for instance, we write MOVE CORRESPONDING A TO B, where A and B are identifiers for groups, e.g. records, subordinate elementary items in A are moved to the corresponding elementary items in B. Two elementary items correspond to each other if they have identical names and also identical qualifiers within A and B, while their order in A and B is not significant. If two corresponding items have different pictures, necessary conversions and editing take place. Thus the effect of a MOVE CORRESPONDING- statement is equivalent to a series of simple MOVE- statements. Items in B that have no counterpart in A are not affected when the CORRESPONDING option is used. It is easy to see that CORRESPONDING makes no sense when A or B are names of elementary items.

The verb EXAMINE is used when we want to process certain characters in a data item. It has the general format:

EXAMINE identifier

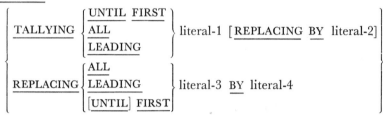

With an EXAMINE-statement we examine the characters of the item from left to right. In each statement we are interested in a particular character, in the format represented by literal-1 or literal-3, and we can count how many times it occurs or replace it by another character. The counting of occurrences is performed in a special register containing 5 digits with the reserved COBOL- name TALLY. We can use the value of TALLY when we have performed an EXAMINE-statement with tallying. We demonstrate the effect of some different EXAMINE-statements with the following examples:

EXAMINE ARTHUR TALLYING ALL "A"

With this statement we count how many A:s occur in the item ARTHUR. If, for instance, ARTHUR contains "ABRACADABRA", TALLY is given the value 5.

EXAMINE BENJAMIN TALLYING LEADING ZEROS REPLACING BY SPACES

Here we count the number of leading zeros in the item BENJAMIN and re- place them by spaces at the same time. If BENJAMIN contains "00012.04", TALLY is given the value 3 and the contents are changed to " 12.04".

EXAMINE CHARLIE TALLYING UNTIL FIRST "."

Here we count all characters preceding the first point. If CHARLIE con- tains "012,356.47", TALLY is given the value 7. If the text REPLACING BY 2 is added to the statement, this has the result that the contents of CHARLIE are changed to "2222222.47".

EXAMINE DAVID REPLACING ALL "L" BY "Z"

114

If DAVID contains "HILLBILLY" the contents are changed to "HIZZBIZZY". TALLY is unaffected. If instead we had written

EXAMINE DAVID REPLACING FIRST "I" BY "E"

we would get "HELLBILLY" after the execution of the statement.

There is one kind of conditions that we have not treated before namely *sign conditions*. A sign condition is used to determine whether the value of a numeric elementary item or an arithmetic expression is positive, negative, or zero. It has the general format:

$$\left\{ \begin{matrix} \text{identifier} \\ \text{arithmetic-expression} \end{matrix} \right\} \text{ IS [NOT]} \left\{ \begin{matrix} \underline{\text{POSITIVE}} \\ \underline{\text{NEGATIVE}} \\ \underline{\text{ZERO}} \end{matrix} \right\}$$

Examples:

SUM-B POSITIVE

X ** 2 + Y ** 2 IS NOT ZERO

Now we are going to describe an abbreviated way of writing compound conditions (cf. 5.6.), which can give more elegant COBOL texts. We name the left member in a relation the subject and the right member the object of the relation. In the relation A GREATER B, A is then the subject and B the object. In a condition consisting of several relations which are connected by the logical operators AND or OR, the relations may have the same subject or have both the relational operator and the subject in common. Examples:

A + B IS GREATER THAN 0 AND A + B IS LESS THAN 100
YEAR IS EQUAL TO 1870 OR YEAR IS EQUAL TO 1914 OR
YEAR IS EQUAL TO 1939

In COBOL we are allowed in such cases to write out only the first relation completely, and then abbreviate the following ones by omitting the subject (and the relational operator), thus implying that it is the same as in the first relation. Examples:

A + B IS GREATER THAN 0 AND LESS THAN 100
YEAR IS EQUAL TO 1870 OR 1914 OR 1939

If, as in the last example, also the same logical operator occurs several times, it is sufficient to write it out for the last occurrence. We are thus allowed to write:

YEAR IS EQUAL TO 1870 1914 OR 1939

It was described in Section 5.6. how it is possible in a PERFORM-statement with the VARYING option to give an item a starting value which later on is modified each time the controlled sequence of statements is executed. This construction can be extended so that two or three numeric elementary items are varied. This is especially useful in processing subscripted data items with several subscripts. Format:

PERFORM procedure-name-1 [THRU procedure-name-2]

$$\text{VARYING identifier-1 FROM} \left\{ \begin{array}{l} \text{identifier-2} \\ \text{integer-2} \end{array} \right\}$$

$$\text{BY} \left\{ \begin{array}{l} \text{identifier-3} \\ \text{integer-3} \end{array} \right\} \text{UNTIL condition-1}$$

$$\text{AFTER identifier-4 FROM} \left\{ \begin{array}{l} \text{identifier-5} \\ \text{integer-5} \end{array} \right\}$$

$$\text{BY} \left\{ \begin{array}{l} \text{identifier-6} \\ \text{integer-6} \end{array} \right\} \text{UNTIL condition-2}$$

$$\text{[AFTER identifier-7 FROM} \left\{ \begin{array}{l} \text{identifier-8} \\ \text{integer-8} \end{array} \right\}$$

$$\text{BY} \left\{ \begin{array}{l} \text{identifier-9} \\ \text{integer-9} \end{array} \right\} \text{UNTIL condition-3]}$$

In an example we shall describe the effect of such a PERFORM-statement, and again we use the expert table of the government of Idyllia in Section 6.6. If we want to compute the number of employees working with investigations, orders, and commands, i.e. to sum all employees in divisions 12 through 15 we can write:

```
INVESTIGATORS. MOVE ZERO TO TOTAL.
    PERFORM SUMMATION VARYING DEPT-NO FROM 1 BY 1
    UNTIL DEPT-NO GREATER 15
    AFTER DIV-NO FROM 12 BY 1
    UNTIL DIV-NO GREATER 15
    AFTER CAT-NO FROM 1 BY 1
    UNTIL CAT-NO GREATER 12.
    . . .
SUMMATION. ADD DIV-EXPERT (DEPT-NO, DIV-NO,
    CAT-NO) TO TOTAL.
```

The PERFORM-statement is equivalent to the following piece of program:

```
    MOVE 1 TO DEPT-NO MOVE 12 TO DIV-NO
    MOVE 1 TO CAT-NO.
11. IF DEPT-NO GREATER 15 GO TO OUT.
12. IF DIV-NO GREATER 15 MOVE 12 TO DIV-NO
    ADD 1 TO DEPT-NO GO TO 11.
13. IF CAT-NO GREATER 12 MOVE 1 TO CAT-NO
    ADD 1 TO DIV-NO GO TO 12.
    PERFORM SUMMATION
    ADD 1 TO CAT-NO GO TO 13.
OUT. . . .
```

Thus, the summation is first performed on category (CAT – NO), then on division (DIV – NO), and finally on department (DEPT – NO). It should be mentioned that all identifiers in the format must correspond to elementary items described as integers and that the value of the varied identifiers always must be positive.

It should be observed that we are permitted to use the same paragraph-name in different sections of the procedure division. If the paragraph-name P2 occurs in more than one section and a paragraph with this name is referred to from its own section, then it is sufficient to write GO TO P2. If it is referred to from another section, however, the paragraph-name must be qualified by the proper section-name. Example:

PERFORM P2 IN ACCOUNTING

We note that the word SECTION is not written in qualified paragraph-names. Regardless of the possibility of making names unique by qualifying it is not permissible to use the same identifier as both data-name and pro-cedure-name in one program.

The verb ALTER provides a means of changing the procedure-name to which a given GO-statement refers. This can be useful if we want to change the structure of the program during execution. If, for instance, the para-graph P1 is written:

P1. GO TO S4.

then the statement

ALTER P1 TO PROCEED TO S2

has the effect that S4 is replaced by S2. A paragraph whose contents are changed by ALTER, must not contain more than one statement.

An interesting feature in COBOL is the possibility of expressing parts of the procedure division in another programming language. In order to proceed from COBOL to the other language we use a statement with the verb ENTER followed by the name of the language in question. After that all statements are regarded as written in this language until a statement ENTER COBOL is detected. From here on the statements are regarded as COBOL statements again. For details about this feature it is necessary to consult the manual of the COBOL system to be used.

In order to indicate that certain paragraphs and sentences in the proce-dure division should be interpreted as comments by the computer, we use the verb NOTE. These comments do not affect the execution of the program but only serve as explanations for a person reading it. If NOTE begins a paragraph all statements in the paragraph are regarded as a comment and are completely ignored in the compilation of the program. If NOTE begins a sentence of another kind the comment ends by the first instance a period followed by a blank is met. In the following example comments have been marked by underlining.

DATA-DESCRIPTION. <u>NOTE A MUST BE EXPRESSED IN HOURS, B IN MINUTES.</u> B = 60 * A.

MAIN-PROGRAM. ADD 1 TO A. <u>NOTE CORRECTION FOR DAYLIGHT SAVING TIME.</u> MOVE ZERO TO B.

In some applications it may be advantageous to be able to alter and enlarge the standard repertory of COBOL for the processing of e.g. magnetic tape files. In such cases we lose the independence of the medium for the file, but gain a better control of what happens when the program is run. Additions to the standard procedures for error handling and labeling can be achieved with the verb USE and further there are some more options for the verbs OPEN and CLOSE.

Here we give the complete format for the verb OPEN regarding sequential files:

$$\underline{\text{OPEN}} \left\{ \begin{array}{l} \underline{\text{INPUT}} \left\{ \text{file-name-1} \left[\dfrac{\text{REVERSED}}{\text{WITH } \underline{\text{NO}} \text{ REWIND}} \right] \right\} \cdots \\ \quad [\underline{\text{OUTPUT}} \ \{\text{file-name-2} \ [\text{WITH } \underline{\text{NO}} \ \underline{\text{REWIND}}] \} \ldots] \\ \underline{\text{OUTPUT}} \ \{\text{file-name-1} \ [\text{WITH } \underline{\text{NO}} \ \underline{\text{REWIND}}]\} \ldots \\ \quad \left[\underline{\text{INPUT}} \left\{ \text{file-name-2} \left[\dfrac{\text{REVERSED}}{\text{WITH } \underline{\text{NO}} \text{ REWIND}} \right] \right\} \cdots \right] \end{array} \right\}$$

There are tape units where it is possible to process the records in reverse order, an option which saves time, especially in connection with certain sorting procedures. If we use REVERSED when such a file is opened we will get the records starting with the last one and then in reversed order. In normal cases the tape is rewound to the beginning when a file is opened. If we want to avoid this we write NO REWIND after the corresponding file-name. Example:

```
OPEN INPUT A-FILE B-FILE NO REWIND
SORTFILE REVERSED
OUTPUT C-FILE NO REWIND D-FILE
```

The format for the verb CLOSE is, more completely:

$$\underline{\text{CLOSE}} \left\{ \text{file-name} \ [\underline{\text{REEL}}] \left[\text{WITH} \left\{ \dfrac{\text{NO REWIND}}{\underline{\text{LOCK}}} \right\} \right] \right\} \cdots$$

For files stored on several magnetic-tape reels, the computer proceeds to the next reel (e.g. by switching over to another tape unit), when the current tape is written full or is read to the end and then ending and beginning label records are written or checked on the tapes. If a CLOSE-statement with the REEL option is encountered on execution of the program, the change of reels takes place before the end of the current tape. This may be useful if we want to provide for a rerun point (cf. 7.1.) or if we want to store certain parts of a file on different magnetic tapes. By NO REWIND we can prevent rewinding of the current tape, if, for instance, we want to read it reversed later on. By the option LOCK we can lock the file so that it cannot be opened again in the same program.

To enlarge the standard procedures for labeling and error handling we can use the verb USE. The time when procedures controlled by this verb are called does not depend on the flow of the COBOL program but on the state of the external units. Therefore a section controlled by a USE-statement must be placed in a special part of the procedure division called the DECLARATIVES-part which is headed by the word DECLARATIVES and terminated by END DECLARATIVES. This part must be written in the beginning of the procedure division, before all other procedures. A section directed by USE can, as usual, contain one or more paragraphs, but the section header must be immediately followed by the USE-statement.

For constructing special error procedures we have the following format:

USE AFTER STANDARD ERROR PROCEDURE ON

$$
\left\{
\begin{array}{l}
\text{file-name-1 [, file-name-2]}\dots \\
\text{INPUT} \\
\text{OUTPUT}
\end{array}
\right\}
$$

It is thus possible to apply the special error procedure to some specified files or to all input or output files.

For construction and checking of labels defined by the programmer we have the following options:

USE $\left\{ \begin{array}{l} \text{BEFORE} \\ \text{AFTER} \end{array} \right\}$ STANDARD $\left[\begin{array}{l} \text{BEGINNING} \\ \text{ENDING} \end{array} \right] \left[\begin{array}{l} \text{REEL} \\ \text{FILE} \end{array} \right]$ LABEL PROCEDURE ON

$$
\left\{
\begin{array}{l}
\text{file-name-1 [, file-name-2]}\dots \\
\text{INPUT} \\
\text{OUTPUT}
\end{array}
\right\}
$$

These USE-statements can also be applied to perform further label handling connected with the normal handling of standard labels. Files with the description LABEL RECORDS ARE OMITTED in the data division cannot be affected by such a USE-statement. If neither BEGINNING nor ENDING are included in the USE-statement the section directed by USE is executed for both beginning and ending labels, and if neither REEL nor FILE are included, it is executed for both tape and file labels.

119

As an example we consider a task which among other things contains reading a file INFILE. If a reading error should occur, all open files are closed and a message is printed by a DISPLAY-statement after which the execution is terminated. The procedure division in the COBOL program can then start as follows:

```
PROCEDURE DIVISION.
DECLARATIVES.
READ-ERROR SECTION. USE AFTER ERROR
     PROCEDURE ON INFILE.
ERROR-PRINT-OUT. CLOSE INFILE, OUTFILE, TRANSAC,
     REPORT-1.
     DISPLAY "READING ERROR IN INFILE.".
     STOP RUN.
END DECLARATIVES.
WORK SECTION.
START. ...
```

It should be noted that the DECLARATIVES-part must be followed by a section header, before the other paragraphs in the procedure division. It should further be observed that it is not permissible to let the statements in the DECLARATIVES-part refer to sections or paragraphs outside this part. The reverse is also true except for references in PERFORM-statements.

9.3. The data division

In this section we are going to deal with a few clauses that can be used instead of the PICTURE-clause to describe the general properties and editing of an elementary item. Further we are going to treat condition-names and the option for copying data descriptions. Finally some clauses for having different data items share the same storage area will be treated.

With the clause

$$\text{CLASS IS} \begin{Bmatrix} \underline{\text{ALPHABETIC}} \\ \underline{\text{NUMERIC}} \\ \underline{\text{ALPHANUMERIC}} \\ \underline{\text{AN}} \end{Bmatrix}$$

we specify to which category an elementary item belongs. AN is an abbreviation for ALPHANUMERIC. The clause can be written at any level. Written at group level it applies to the elementary items of the group, while the group itself is treated as alphanumeric. If no category has been given and the elementary item is not described with USAGE IS COMPUTATIONAL, then the class of the elementary item is assumed to be alphanumeric.

In order to specify the size of an elementary item without the PICTURE-clause we can use one of the two formats

120

$$\underline{\text{SIZE}} \text{ IS integer} \begin{bmatrix} \text{CHARACTERS} \\ \text{DIGITS} \end{bmatrix}$$

$$\underline{\text{SIZE}} \text{ IS integer-1 } \underline{\text{TO}} \text{ integer-2} \begin{bmatrix} \text{CHARACTERS} \\ \text{DIGITS} \end{bmatrix}$$

[$\underline{\text{DEPENDING}}$ ON data-name]

In the first format the integer specifies the number of character positions to be reserved in the storage for the item. The required storage area for an elementary item in a file can vary considerably in many applications. A way of solving this problem is to define the elementary item in such a way that it can accomodate data of maximum size all the time. However, there are occasions when it is necessary to use the storage area in external units in an efficient manner, and then we can use the second format to specify elementary items of *variable size*. As an example we consider the description of the alphabetic elementary item NAME which has a size varying from 5 to 40 positions:

```
0 2   NAME  SIZE  IS  5  TO  40  ALPHABETIC  CHARACTERS .
```

It is permissible to insert category (ALPHABETIC, etc.) and usage (COMPUTATIONAL or DISPLAY) clauses immediately before CHARACTERS (or DIGITS). If DEPENDING is included the size of the elementary item is determined by the succeeding data-name. Example:

```
0 1   RECORD-1 .
      0 2  NUMBER-C  SIZE  IS  2  COMPUTATIONAL  DIGITS .
      0 2  NAME  SIZE  IS  5  TO  40  ALPHABETIC  CHARACTERS
      DEPENDING  ON  NUMBER-C .
```

It is also possible to specify variable size by a PICTURE-clause which is indicated by inserting the letter L in front of the picture. The maximum size is then given by a picture in the usual way. With PICTURE the two examples above can be written as follows:

```
0 2   NAME  PICTURE  IS  LA ( 4 0 ) .
0 1   RECORD-1 .
      0 2  NUMBER-C  PICTURE  IS  99  COMPUTATIONAL .
      0 2  NAME  PICTURE  IS  LA ( 4 0 )  DEPENDING  ON
      NUMBER-C .
```

If we want to specify also the minimum size, then we must use a construction containing a SIZE-clause:

```
0 2   NAME  PICTURE  IS  LA ( 4 0 )  SIZE  IS  5 .
```

It should be observed that elementary items of variable size cannot be edited or subscripted.

The appearance of an operational sign is specified by the clause

SIGNED

while the position of the assumed decimal point is indicated by

$$\text{POINT LOCATION IS} \left\{ \begin{array}{l} \underline{\text{LEFT}} \\ \underline{\text{RIGHT}} \end{array} \right\} \text{integer PLACES}$$

We demonstrate the application of these clauses in some examples where we also give equivalent PICTURE descriptions of the elementary items:

```
02   I SIZE IS 5 NUMERIC DIGITS
     POINT LOCATION IS LEFT 2 PLACES.
02   I PICTURE IS 999V99.
02   J NUMERIC SIZE 4 POINT LEFT 7 SIGNED.
02   J PICTURE SPPP9999.
02   K SIZE IS 3 COMPUTATIONAL DIGITS
     POINT RIGHT 2 SIGNED.
02   K PICTURE S999PP COMPUTATIONAL.
```

We use the following clause for editing:

$$\left[; \left\{ \begin{array}{l} \underline{\text{ZERO}} \ \text{SUPPRESS} \\ \underline{\text{CHECK}} \ \text{PROTECT} \\ \underline{\text{FLOAT}} \left\{ \begin{array}{l} \underline{\text{DOLLAR}} \\ \underline{\text{CURRENCY}} \end{array} \right\} \underline{\text{SIGN}} \end{array} \right\} [\underline{\text{LEAVING}} \ \text{integer PLACES}] \right]$$

$$[\underline{\text{BLANK}} \ \text{WHEN} \ \underline{\text{ZERO}}]$$

The alternatives ZERO SUPPRESS and CHECK PROTECT mean that leading zeros are to be replaced by blanks and asterisks respectively, while the FLOAT SIGN option specifies insertion of a currency sign in the position of the rightmost suppressed character. LEAVING is used to terminate the suppression of zeros before the assumed decimal point is encountered. Here we give some examples of editing using editing clauses and equivalent PICTURE-clauses:

```
04   SUM-1 SIZE IS 7 NUMERIC DISPLAY DIGITS
     POINT LOCATION IS LEFT 2 PLACES
     ZERO SUPPRESS LEAVING 3 PLACES.
04   SUM-1 PICTURE IS ZZ999V99.
02   WEEKLY-PAY SIZE IS 6 NUMERIC DISPLAY DIGITS
     POINT LOCATION IS LEFT 2 PLACES CHECK PROTECT.
02   WEEKLY-PAY PICTURE IS ****V99.
```

BLANK WHEN ZERO means that if the data item has the value zero, then only spaces are to be stored. However, editing where zeros are replaced by asterisks is not affected. The option BLANK WHEN ZERO is of special interest since this editing option cannot be achieved by the PICTURE-clause. Examples:

```
0 3   A  PICTURE  IS  9 9 9 9  BLANK  WHEN  ZERO.
0 3   B  PICTURE  IS  + + + 9 9 . 9 9  BLANK  WHEN  ZERO.
0 3   C  SIZE  IS  7  NUMERIC  DIGITS  POINT  LEFT  4
      FLOAT  SIGN  BLANK  WHEN  ZERO.
```

It should be observed that A is regarded as a numeric edited elementary item and hence it is not possible to use it in arithmetic operations in the procedure division.

Occasionally an elementary item in a record is not used by the COBOL program. In such cases it is not necessary to give the item a data-name, but the key word FILLER is written in the position of the data-name. Such elementary items cannot be referred to, and their contents can be reached only indirectly through higher level items. For example, the program in Section 8.1. contains a description of a record TR with an elementary item OCC – NO which is not used in the program. Instead of using the data-name we could replace it by FILLER. However, this possibility is particularly advantageous when several consecutive elementary items are not used in a program. In the example below we assume that for a number of individuals we have recorded 20 different properties, each specified by a digit or a letter. If in a special program the properties Nos. 2, 3, and 17 are to be investigated, then the following record description is sufficient.

```
0 1   INDIVIDUAL.
      0 2   NR  PICTURE  9 9 9 9 .
      0 2   FILLER  PICTURE  X .
      0 2   PROPERTY - 2  PICTURE  A .
      0 2   PROPERTY - 3  PICTURE  A .
      0 2   FILLER  PICTURE  X ( 1 3 ) .
      0 2   PROPERTY - 1 7  PICTURE  9 .
      0 2   FILLER  PICTURE  XXX .
```

In Section 4.6. we mentioned the possibility to name conditions by *condition-names*. Each condition-name is associated with a data item and a set of values which this item can assume. The data item is called a *conditional variable*. A condition associated with a conditional variable is defined in the data division by the format:

$$88 \text{ condition-name}; \left\{ \begin{array}{l} \underline{\text{VALUE}} \text{ IS} \\ \underline{\text{VALUES}} \text{ ARE} \end{array} \right\} \text{literal-1} [\underline{\text{THRU}} \text{ literal-2}]$$

$$[, \text{literal-3} [\underline{\text{THRU}} \text{ literal-4}]]\ldots.$$

This construction is written immediately after the entry of the conditional variable. The level number 88 indicates that the description applies to a

123

condition. Literal-1, literal-2, etc. must be values that the conditional variable can assume. THRU is used to define a range of values belonging to the condition-name. Example:

```
04    YEAR-OF-STUDY  PICTURE  99.
   88    COMPREHENSIVE-SCHOOL  VALUES  ARE  1  THRU  9.
   88    LOWER-DIVISION  VALUES  ARE  1,  2,  3.
   88    MIDDLE-DIVISION  VALUE  4  THRU  6.
   88    UPPER-DIVISION  VALUES  7,  8,  9.
   88    CONTINUATION-SCHOOL  VALUES  10,  11.
   88    ERROR-IN-CODE  VALUES  ARE  ZERO,
         12  THRU  99.
```

If, in the procedure division, we write for instance IF MIDDLE – DIVISION GO TO P2, it is tested whether the value of YEAR – OF – STUDY is 4, 5, or 6. If this is the case, a jump to P2 is performed. Note that also the condition-name COMPREHENSIVE – SCHOOL at that time has the value true. Obviously it is possible to assign the same value to more than one condition-name. We give two further examples:

```
04    PAY-CATEGORY  PICTURE  IS  A  OCCURS  5  TIMES.
   88    PIECE-WAGES  VALUE  IS  "P".
   88    HOURLY-WAGES  VALUE  IS  "H".
   88    MONTHLY-SALARY  VALUE  IS  "M".
   88    ERROR-IN-CODE  VALUE  IS  SPACE,
         "A"  THRU  "G",  "I"  THRU  "L",  "N",  "O",
         "Q"  THRU  "Z".

03    A.
   88    CATEGORY  VALUES  SPACES  THRU  "MMM777".
   04    B  PICTURE  AAA.
   04    C  PICTURE  XXX.
```

When the conditional variable is subscripted, then the condition-name must also be subscripted, and the same combination of subscripts has to be used, e.g. HOURLY – WAGES (4). As is the case for data-names, condition-names may be qualified by the name of the conditional variable and its superior data items, e.g. CATEGORY IN A.

The examples of COBOL programs in Chapter 8 suggest that different records or parts of records often have identical descriptions. In order to reduce the amount of work in writing the data division, we can use the COPY-clause and copy the description of one data item onto another. Entries containing COPY have the format:

level-number data-name-1 COPY data-name-2 [FROM LIBRARY].

During compilation of the COBOL program the COPY-clause is replaced by the clauses following the data-name in the entry of data-name-2. Further, the descriptions of the data items subordinate to data-name-2 are inserted. During the replacement all level numbers are adjusted in such a way that the difference between the level number of data-name-2 and data-name-1 is subtracted. The level numbers 66 and 88, however, are left unchanged. Example:

```
0 1    A .
       0 2    B   PICTURE   9 9 .
       0 2    C   COPY   G .
              0 4    D   PICTURE   XX .
0 1    E .
       0 7    F   PICTURE   9 9 V 9 .
       0 7    G   OCCURS   3   TIMES .
              0 9    H   PICTURE   9 9 9 .
              0 9    I .
                     1 1    J   PICTURE   X ( 7 ) .
                     1 1    K   PICTURE   S 9 9 V 9 9 .
```

The description of the record A after the copying is as follows:

```
0 1    A .
       0 2    B   PICTURE   9 9 .
       0 2    C   OCCURS   3   TIMES .
              0 4    H   PICTURE   9 9 9 .
              0 4    I .
                     0 6    J   PICTURE   X ( 7 ) .
                     0 6    K   PICTURE   S 9 9 V 9 9 .
              0 4    D   PICTURE   XX .
```

Since the data-names of the inserted entries occur in two places, we have to use qualified data-names when referring to them, e.g. K IN C (2) or K IN G (2). Further we have to check that data items subordinate to the item with the COPY-clause, get permissible level numbers and that the record gets the intended hierarchical structure. For instance, in the example we are not allowed to give D the level number 03. If the data item with COPY has the level number equal to 66 or 88, the level number of data-name-2 must be the same. We are now going to demonstrate how COPY can be used in the examples of Chapter 8. In the program of Section 8.1., we can describe the record NEW by

```
0 1    NEW   COPY   OLD .
```

The description of the record NP in Section 8.3. can be replaced by

```
0 1    NP   COPY   OP .
```

The last part of the format, FROM LIBRARY, suggests another function of COPY, namely retrieving data descriptions from a COBOL library. For the copying the same rules are valid with respect to level numbers and so on as has been described before. The use of a COBOL library is discussed in more detail in Section 9.4.

By the data description entry

66 data-name-1 RENAMES data-name-2 [THRU data-name-3] .

we can define a comprehensive data-name for a number of elementary items belonging to different groups in the hierarchical structure. Entries containing RENAMES are written after all other entries in the record. Data-name-3 must not be subordinate to data-name-2. If both data-name-2 and data-name-3 are elementary items, they as well as all elementary items in between belong to the group data-name-1; if they are groups all elementary items, from the first one in data-name-2 through the last one in data-name-3, belong to data-name-1. The new group must not contain all the elementary items of the record. Example:

```
0 1    A   . . .
       0 2    B   . . .
       0 2    C   . . .
              0 3    D   . . .
              0 3    E   . . .
                     0 4    F   . . .
       0 2    H   . . .
       0 2    I   . . .
6 6    J   RENAMES   C   THRU   I .
6 6    K   RENAMES   B   THRU   H .
6 6    L   RENAMES   F   THRU   H .
```

In this example the group J contains the elementary items D, F, H, I. The group K contains B, D, F, H, and finally L the elementary items F and H. Data-name-1 cannot be used as a qualifier, but can itself be qualified by the file-name or record-name; no data-names can be subscripted. When THRU data-name-3 does not occur, the clause defines an alternative data-name for the item. This option can be used, for instance, when we want to avoid long qualified data-names in the procedure division.

Finally we are going to consider an option which makes it possible to store several data items in the same storage area. Then the new description of the storage area is specified by an entry starting as follows:

level-number data-name-1; REDEFINES data-name-2

This entry must be written immediately after the description of the data item (data-name-2) which is given a new data-name (data-name-1) and a new description. The latter one must follow after the REDEFINES-clause. Example:

```
0 1    ARTICLE .
       0 2    TITLE .
              0 3    AUTHOR  PICTURE  A ( 4 0 ) .
              0 3    SUBTITLE  PICTURE  X ( 1 0 0 ) .
       0 2    CHARACTER - GROUP  REDEFINES  TITLE .
              0 3    CHAR  PICTURE  X  OCCURS  1 4 0  TIMES .
```

With this record description we can refer in the procedure division either to the elementary items AUTHOR and SUBTITLE or to the single characters in these two items. As another example we demonstrate that it is possible to use REDEFINES to give starting values to subscripted elementary items defined in the working-storage section or the constant section. As was pointed out in Section 6.8. it is not permissible to apply the VALUE-clause to subscripted elementary items. In this example, for instance, AVERAGE (3) has the value 127.94 when the execution of the procedure division starts.

```
01    TABULAR-VALUES.
      02    NO-1  PICTURE  S999V99  VALUE  IS  -112.31.
      02    NO-2  PICTURE  S999V99  VALUE  IS  10.13.
      02    NO-3  PICTURE  S999V99  VALUE  IS  127.94.
      02    NO-4  PICTURE  S999V99  VALUE  IS  712.26.
01    TABLE  REDEFINES  TABULAR-VALUES.
      02    AVERAGE  PICTURE  S999V99  OCCURS  4  TIMES.
```

It is not possible to use REDEFINES on level 01 in the file section. Further, data-name-1 and data-name-2 must have the same level number and the same size. Data-name-2 must not be subscripted, and the new description must not contain VALUE- clauses assigning starting values to the data items.

9.4. The COBOL library

When we use a computer, it is very often the case that certain subproblems occur in different places and can be described by identical program texts. We have seen that the same data description can be employed in several places in the data division by using the COPY-clause in order to reduce the writing effort. When program texts are common to several programs there is an option to store them in a COBOL library on an external unit, from which they can be included in the source program during the compilation. The rules concerning the construction and maintenance of a COBOL library are different for different machines. An advantage with a library is that, as a rule, the texts stored in it are correct, an ideal state which is often very difficult to reach in individual programs. The COBOL library may contain texts which can be included in both the environment division, the data division, and the procedure division of a program.

Information about the paragraphs of the environment division is retrieved from the library to the COBOL program by the construction

COPY library-name

after the paragraph-name instead of ordinary entries. The library-name is formed in the same way as a data-name and identifies a certain program text in the library. Examples:

```
SOURCE-COMPUTER.  COPY  S-C-STANDARD.
OBJECT-COMPUTER.  COPY  ENV-LIB-12.
SPECIAL-NAMES.  COPY  STANDARD-FOR-PRINTER.
FILE-CONTROL.  COPY  INVENTORY-FILES.
I-O-CONTROL.  COPY  I-O-C-4.
```

The COPY-clause is also used in the data division, and then it is placed after file-names and data-names, respectively. There is a difference between the use of the clause on the file description level and on lower levels. In the first case the library-name identifies a file description entry. Example:

```
FD  CUSTOMERS  COPY  FD-2-FOR-INVOICING.
```

In the latter case the library-name identifies the description of a record or a data item. Here it is necessary to add FROM LIBRARY to the COPY-clause in order to distinguish this kind of copying from copying a text in the data division (cf. 9.3.). When referring to a data-name in the library on a level lower than the record level, the data-name must be qualified by its record-name. Examples:

```
01  CUSTOMER  COPY  LIBR-CUSTOMER  FROM  LIBRARY.
05  TIME  COPY  MINUTES  IN  MASTER  FROM  LIBRARY.
```

In order to include a text from the library into the procedure division we use the statement

INCLUDE procedure-name

The text may consist of a paragraph or a section which is stored in the library. When a paragraph is copied, the INCLUDE-statement must be the only statement in a paragraph of the COBOL program and this is replaced on compilation by the library routine. In the same way, when a section is copied, the INCLUDE-statement must be the only statement in the corresponding section of the COBOL program. Example:

```
M-S.  INCLUDE  COMPUTE-MONTHLY-SALARIES.
T-C  SECTION.
P.  INCLUDE  TAX-CALCULATION.
```

There is also an option to replace names in the library program by names which are better adjusted to the problem on hand by an addition to the INCLUDE-statement. Example:

```
P1.  INCLUDE  PAY-COMPUTATION  REPLACING
     NAME  BY  AGENT,  ADDR  BY  INTELLIGENCE-NO.
```

Using this option we can choose e.g. data-names in our program independently of the names used in the library.

128

9.5. Segmentation

Every computer has a limited storage capacity and even if the internal storage is large, it is not unusual to encounter programs which are still larger. In such cases we must rely on some kind of *segmentation*. This is generally accomplished by selecting certain program parts to be stored on an external unit. These parts are then brought to the central processor each time they are to be used. Different parts can then use the same space in the internal storage. However, it is necessary to build up the program in such a way that frequent transfers are avoided as far as possible.

COBOL gives a convenient possibility of segmentation as regards the procedure division which must then be divided into sections. Each section is given a priority number which is written immediately after the word SECTION in the section header. Sections having the same priority number will then together form a segment. Segments having the numbers 0—49 form a *fixed portion* of the program, and segments with the numbers 50—99 are *independent segments*. If there is not space enough in the internal storage, a necessary number of independent segments are stored on an external unit, and segments with a high priority number are then taken into consideration first. When such a segment is called in the procedure division it is always assumed to be in its initial state.

If there is not even space for the fixed portion of the program, we can divide the fixed portion into *permanent segments* and *overlayable fixed segments,* using a SEGMENT – LIMIT-option in the environment division. The permanent segments are all the time in a fixed place of the internal storage, while the overlayable ones if necessary can be overlaid by other segments. The overlayable segments, however, are treated as if they always were in the storage. Hence, when they are called again they are in the same state as when they were last used. For this reason it is necessary to save certain information with respect to the state of an overlayable fixed segment. This is done automatically whenever it is overlaid by another segment. For instance, we might need addresses for return jumps in PERFORM-statements or addresses in GO-statements initiated by the verb ALTER. If, for instance, in the OBJECT – COMPUTER-paragraph in the environment division we add the clause SEGMENT – LIMIT IS 37, all segments with priority numbers 0—36 are regarded as permanent segments, all with numbers 37—49 as overlayable fixed segments, and all with numbers 50—99 as independent segments. If no SEGMENT – LIMIT is given, all segments with priority numbers 0—49 are permanent segments.

9.6. Random access

The features of COBOL intended for random access storages, for sorting, and for report writing have not yet been implemented on computers to any large extent. However, the technical development suggests that at least facilities for random access will be available in future COBOL systems. A random access storage is characterized by the fact that the access time is quite independent of which part of the storage is used. In many applications it is advantageous to read or write records in an order independent of how they are stored in the external storage. In such cases it is also natural to use the same file for both reading and writing. We have then to introduce a new feature in the processing of files: the address in the external storage of the record to be processed next must be given by the programmer. Therefore, there is an option in the environment division to connect fixed address registers with data-names in the data division where we can then store current addresses by statements in the procedure division.

For a random access file we add in the FILE – CONTROL-paragraph of the environment division a clause with the format:

ACCESS MODE IS RANDOM, PROCESSING MODE IS SEQUENTIAL,
ACTUAL KEY IS data-name

This format can be modified or combined with other options which cannot be treated here. We point out that a random access file does not have a logical end, and for this reason reading cannot be terminated by an AT END-condition. On the other hand in the format for the verb READ we can replace AT END imperative-statement by INVALID KEY imperative-statement in order to stop the reading when an invalid address has been reached. It should be mentioned that files stored in a random access storage can also be treated in the normal sequential manner. The complete COBOL language also contains options for multiprogramming (random processing) so that several records from random access storages can be processed simultaneously.

9.7. Sorting

In practice sorting is often achieved by special standard routines which are not connected with COBOL. When we want to use the options for sorting in COBOL we have to describe a *sort file* in a special file description entry having the level indicator SD. Sort files contain ordinary data records and the sort file description contains references to subsequent record descriptions which are written in the conventional way. When an ordinary already given file is to be sorted, its contents can be copied on a sort file.

It is also possible to form a sort file in a special part of the procedure division consisting of one or more sections. Records are written on a sort file by use of the verb RELEASE instead of WRITE. When the sorting is completed the records can again be copied on an ordinary file or be taken care of in some other way. When a record is read from a sort file the verb RETURN is used instead of READ.

As an example we are going to demonstrate how we can use the COBOL sorting feature to sort the results produced by the program for indexing of newspaper articles in Section 8.2. We then add to the data division of the program a description of a sort file with the level indicator SD (= Sort file Description) as follows:

```
SD   SORT-FILE DATA RECORD IS SORT-RECORD.
01   SORT-RECORD.
     02 KEY-WORD PICTURE X(24).
     02 TITLE PICTURE X(150).
     02 IDT PICTURE 9(6).
```

The data items of SORT – RECORD in SORT – FILE as well as in OUTPUT – FILE have the same size and position with respect to each other, since OUTPUT – FILE is to be copied on SORT – FILE. Further we must describe another file ARTICLE – INDEX for storing the sorted records. It is described in an ordinary file description with the level indicator FD, and its record description must correspond to the description of SORT – RECORD above. SORT – FILE as well as ARTICLE – INDEX must be associated with external units in the environment division of the program.

By use of the verb SORT in the procedure division we get a complete sorting of a sort file. Immediately before STOP RUN in the program we could add a SORT-statement as follows:

```
SORT SORT-FILE ON ASCENDING KEY KEY-WORD IN
SORT-FILE ON DESCENDING KEY IDT IN SORT-FILE
USING OUTPUT-FILE GIVING ARTICLE-INDEX.
```

Here we have assumed that sorting primarily is to be done according to KEY – WORD IN SORT – FILE on ascending values of keys and secondarily according to IDT IN SORT – FILE on descending values. The list of sorting keys can be of arbitrary length. USING and GIVING indicate the copying of files before and after the sorting process. It is also possible to replace USING file-name and GIVING file-name by INPUT PROCEDURE section-name-1 [THRU section-name-2] and OUTPUT PROCEDURE section-name-1 [THRU section-name-2], respectively. Here we refer to the program sections mentioned above for forming a sort file and transforming a sorted file.

9.8. Report writing

In many commercial applications it is very important that the result produced by the computer is given an attractive form. Examples of such results are invoices, earnings statements, and premium bills. The print-out from the computer is normally effected by a line printer on special forms adjusted to the size of lines and columns of the printer. According to the features of COBOL discussed up till now, lines with different kinds of print-out must be described as different records in the data division. Further, a detailed editing with blanks must be specified to produce proper spaces between the printed data items. Change of line and page must be ordered from the procedure division. However, in the complete COBOL there is an option to assemble independent data items into a *report* describing clearly the arrangement of the items on the form. We then use the fact that a file, apart from records, also may contain reports which are given names in the file description entry using the following format:

$$\begin{Bmatrix} \underline{\text{REPORT}} \text{ IS} \\ \underline{\text{REPORTS}} \text{ ARE} \end{Bmatrix} \text{ report-name-1 } [, \text{ report-name-2}] \dots$$

The corresponding *report descriptions* are written in a special section headed by REPORT SECTION at the end of the data division. The same report-name may occur in different file descriptions. A report can contain three different types of *report groups* built up by data items, viz. *headings, details,* and *footings.* Headings and footings are automatically printed out, e.g. at the beginning or at the end of the report, at the top or at the bottom of a page, or when certain other conditions are fulfilled. The print-out of details is ordered from the procedure division.

The printing of a report is initiated from the procedure division by INITIATE report-name which resets counters etc. With a statement, GENERATE detail-name, a detail group is printed out. The first time GENERATE is used also certain headings are printed. When the last detail has been printed the report is terminated by TERMINATE report-name which can give print-out of certain footings.

We now give an example of a report description and demonstrate a scheme for the print-out of invoices. We assume that each invoice is limited to one page and can be regarded as a report. The invoice starts by a heading containing name and address of the customer on line 4 and line 6. Beginning with line 12 the details of the invoice are to appear one on each line. Each detail consists of quantity, description of goods, price per item, and price. Two lines after the last detail an automatically computed total price is to appear in the price column preceded by the word "TOTAL".

```
DATA  DIVISION.
FILE  SECTION.
FD  OUT-FILE;  ...  REPORT  IS  INVOICE.
   .
   .
   .
REPORT  SECTION.
RD    INVOICE;  CONTROL  IS  FINAL.
01    CUSTOMER;  TYPE  IS  REPORT  HEADING;
      NEXT  GROUP  11.
      02  LINE  4;  COLUMN  6;  PICTURE  X(30);
          SOURCE  NAME.
      02  LINE  6;  COLUMN  6;  PICTURE  X(30);
          SOURCE  ADDR.
01    DETAIL-ENTRY;  TYPE  IS  DETAIL;  LINE  PLUS  1.
      02  COLUMN  2;  PICTURE  ZZ;  SOURCE  QUANTITY.
      02  COLUMN  6;  PICTURE  X(24);
          SOURCE  DESCRIPTION.
      02  COLUMN  32;  PICTURE  ZZZ.ZZ;
          SOURCE  PRICE-PER-ITEM.
      02  COLUMN  40;  PICTURE  ZZZZ.ZZ;  SOURCE  PRICE.
01    TOTAL;  TYPE  IS  CONTROL  FOOTING  FINAL;
      LINE  PLUS  2.
      02  COLUMN  32;  PICTURE  X(5);  VALUE  "TOTAL".
      02  COLUMN  39;  PICTURE  Z(5).ZZ;  SUM  PRICE.
```

A report description entry starts with the level indicator RD (= Report Description) and the name of the report. In the example above we also find the clause CONTROL IS FINAL which indicates that the problem involves automatic summation. After that the report groups are described, each type starting on level 01. CUSTOMER is a report heading, DETAIL – ENTRY is a detail, and TOTAL is a control footing; in the latter the automatic summation is applied. The heading is printed on the first execution of the statement GENERATE DETAIL – ENTRY in the procedure division, while TOTAL is printed on the execution of TERMINATE INVOICE. The report heading consists of a name and an address written on line 4 and line 6, respectively, beginning at column 6. There are 30 character positions reserved for each of these items. The current values are taken from NAME and ADDR, respectively, which have to be described in some other section of the data division. After the printing the paper is advanced to the 11th line (NEXT GROUP 11). Before each detail group is printed the paper is to be advanced one line (LINE PLUS 1). Starting columns for the data items have been specified and the data description with PICTURE works in the ordinary way so that the SOURCE items are edited before they are transferred to the report. The control footing is written two lines below the last detail. Its second item has worked as a summation register where the prices of the detail entries have been accumulated after every execution of GENERATE.

Chapter 10. COBOL on computer

ccasionally the question arises as to what criteria should govern the optimal exploitation of computers. One may still meet the attitude, even at the highest administrative levels, that one should try to minimize the cost for computer time. The authors of this book want to make clear that they do not support this idea, which they believe is an excellent example of sub-optimization. Obviously, computers have not been built to be used as little as possible but to relieve people of strenuous and tedious routine work. From this point of view it would be much more reasonable to minimize human labour. As computers are becoming faster and cheaper, this criterion seems to become more and more reasonable. However, since many computers are still relatively slow it is sensible to discuss simple means to keep the machine time within moderate limits.

One simple measure can be taken when the problem is formulated: to examine critically whether parts of the program are even necessary. Data of sometimes rather questionable value, are often routinely produced just because "they might be nice to have". Also the quality of the original data is of great importance, and as a rule it will pay to do a good job of generating "clean" data.

During execution of programs, the file handling is particularly time-consuming, and in general one ought to keep the number of passages as low as possible. It may also be worth-while to consider how the updating of a file should be organized or how long a correction file should be used. A well-planned data description is of highest significance for an efficient program. In order to avoid duplication of programming effort, it is advantageous to store descriptions of files intended for several different programs in a COBOL library.

Storing on magnetic tapes is usually done by grouping several records into a block which is specified by the programmer in the file description.

Between any two adjacent blocks on the magnetic tape there is a gap. Blocking of records saves tape as more records can then be put on one reel. It also saves computer time since whole blocks are read one at a time. If the records are already very large, only small gains are possible from the blocking, however. For computers with a very small internal memory the size of available storage must sometimes be taken into account on defining the records of a file; otherwise a record may be so large that it cannot be accomodated in the memory.

In many cases the programmer can choose between different data representations, and it might be well worth to consider carefully which is the best form (cf. e.g. USAGE COMPUTATIONAL vs USAGE DISPLAY) as a conversion in one direction or other may be rather time-consuming. The clause SYNCHRONIZED speeds up computation but at the price of using more memory space.

Also one ought to organize the computational work in such a way that no operations are repeated unnecessarily. If, for example, the expression $X = (A+B)^3 - 6(A+B)^2 + 7(A+B) - 8$ is to be evaluated, then it is advisable first to compute $C = A + B$ and then $X = ((C-6) * C + 7) * C - 8$. Further, computations with simple variables are almost always faster than computations with subscripted variables. If the value of a subscripted variable is used several times in a computation it is suitable to assign this value to an auxiliary simple variable. An example of this technique is shown in the program in Section 8.2. where the auxiliary variable T is used.

Further it should be mentioned that much more programming work is spent on programs intended to be used for a long period of time than on one-shot programs. Often problems in administrative data processing belong to the former group.

In practice it is almost inevitable that all COBOL programs initially contain a number of errors, and the use of a program for production runs must be preceded by a testing and debugging period. In a first phase the COBOL compiler will analyze the program and produce an error list of violations of the COBOL rules. When all grammatical errors have been corrected, the object program is generated and after that it is wise to test the program for possible logical errors. This can be done by having the program process a set of test-data for which the correct results have been determined manually. Test-data should be chosen in such a way that each part of the program will be used in the test. Further it is important to check the files which are formed during execution of the program. Conveniently, files on magnetic tape may be printed out separately by use of standard tape dump programs. In order to facilitate correction of a program it is often practical to start each statement on a new line, especially when the program is punched on cards.

Implementation of COBOL has been performed for the majority of the large computer systems on the market. The very first compilers seem to have been subject to deficiencies almost throughout, but nowadays most of them are acceptable, even if the quality varies. Space limitations make it impossible to describe occurring differences, and we restrict ourselves to pointing at the importance of consulting the manuals of the system to be used.

Almost all current COBOL systems have implemented only a subset of COBOL-65. For attaining as large a compatibility as possible between different systems several groups are now working on standardization of different subsets of the language. So far (December 1967) no such standard forms have been confirmed. However, by January 1967 USASI presented a proposal for a standard in which the language elements are organized into functional processing modules. To a certain module are then assigned those language elements which correspond to a certain function with respect to application. There are altogether eight different modules, viz. table handling (subscripting and indexing), sequential access, random access, random processing, sort, report writer, segmentation, and library. The language elements which are concerned with the internal processing (arithmetic, transfers, flow control, etc.) form a nucleus of the language. The nucleus is divided into two, and the modules into two or three levels. Throughout, a lower level is a proper subset of the next higher level within the same module; this also holds for the nucleus. An implementation of COBOL which includes a certain level in each module and the nucleus, is considered as a STANDARD COBOL. For example, the minimum standard consists of the lowest level in the nucleus, in table handling, and in sequential access; in the other modules the lowest level is empty. It is impracticable to try to give a detailed description of the contents of all levels. However, it could be mentioned that the proposed full USASI STANDARD COBOL by itself is a subset of COBOL-65. Language elements considered less useful have been omitted together with such elements as are too expensive to implement or only represent alternative means of expression. Examples of the latter kind are the alternatives to the PICTURE-clause as described in Section 9.3.

136

Literature

1. Brinch Hansen, P., and House, R.: The COBOL Compiler for the Siemens 3003. BIT 6,1 (1966), 1—23.
2. COBOL, Edition 1965. Department of Defence, Washington, 1965.
3. COBOL Language Subcommittee of CODASYL, Page changes to COBOL Edition 1965 up to January 1, 1967. COBOL Information Bulletin no. 10, Nov., 1967.
4. Conway, M. E.: Design of a Separable Transition-Diagram Compiler. Comm. ACM 6,7 (July, 1963), 396—408.
5. Conway, M. E., and Speroni, J.: Arithmetizing Declarations, An Application to COBOL. Comm. ACM 5,1 (Jan., 1962), 24—27.
6. Cunningham, J. F., Sammet, J. E., etc.: COBOL Papers. Comm. ACM 5,5 (May, 1962), 236—279.
7. Farina, M. V.: COBOL Simplified. Prentice-Hall, Englewood Cliffs, 1968.
8. Formal Definition of the Syntax of COBOL (preliminary edition). ECMA, Aug., 1967.
9. Kreis, P.: COBOL, Lehrbuch zum Selbstunterricht, Oldenbourg, München, 1967.
10. McCameron, F. A.: COBOL logic and programming. Irwin, Homewood, 1966.
11. McCracken, D. D.: A guide to COBOL programming. Wiley, New York, 1963.
12. Raun, D. L.: An introduction to COBOL computer programming for accounting and business analysis. Dickenson, Belmont, 1966.
13. Report to Conference on Data Systems Languages Including Extended Specifications for a Common Business Oriented Language (COBOL). Department of Defence, Washington, 1962.
14. Report to Conference on Data Systems Languages Including Revised Specifications for a Common Business Oriented Language (COBOL). Department of Defence, Washington, 1961.
15. Rosen, S. (Ed.), Programming systems and languages. McGraw-Hill, New York, 1967.
16. Saxon, J. A.: COBOL, A Self-Instructional Manual. Prentice-Hall, Englewood Cliffs, 1963.
17. USASI Working Group X.3.4.4 Cobol Standards: Proposed USASI COBOL Standard. COBOL Information Bulletin no. 9, April, 1967.
18. Wegner, P. (Ed.): Introduction to System Programming. Academic Press, London, 1964.

Reserved COBOL words

ABOUT
ACCEPT
ACCESS
ACTUAL
ADD
ADDRESS
ADVANCING
AFTER
ALL
ALPHABETIC
ALPHANUMERIC
ALTER
ALTERNATE
AN
AND
APPLY
ARE
AREA
AREAS
ASCENDING
ASSIGN
AT
AUTHOR

BEFORE
BEGINNING
BITS
BLANK
BLOCK
BY

CF
CH
CHARACTERS
CHECK
CLASS
CLOCK – UNITS
CLOSE
COBOL
CODE
COLUMN
COMMA
COMPUTATIONAL
COMPUTE
CONFIGURATION
CONSTANT
CONTAINS
CONTROL
CONTROLS

CONVERSION
COPY
CORRESPONDING
CURRENCY

DATA
DATE – COMPILED
DATE – WRITTEN
DE
DECIMAL – POINT
DECLARATIVES
DEFINE
DEPENDING
DESCENDING
DETAIL
DIGITS
DISPLAY
DIVIDE
DIVIDED
DIVISION
DOLLAR
DOWN

ELSE
END
ENDING
ENTER
ENVIRONMENT
EQUAL
EQUALS
ERROR
EVERY
EXAMINE
EXCEEDS
EXIT
EXPONENTIATED

FD
FILE
FILE – CONTROL
FILE – LIMIT
FILE – LIMITS
FILLER
FINAL
FIRST
FLOAT
FOOTING
FOR
FORMAT
FROM

GENERATE
GIVING
GO
GREATER
GROUP

HASHED
HEADING
HIGH – VALUE
HIGH – VALUES
HOLD

I – O
I – O – CONTROL
IDENTIFICATION
IF
IN
INCLUDE
INDEX
INDEXED
INDICATE
INITIATE
INPUT
INPUT – OUTPUT
INSTALLATION
INTO
INVALID
IS

JUSTIFIED

KEY
KEYS

LABEL
LAST
LEADING
LEAVING
LEFT
LESS
LIBRARY
LIMIT
LIMITS
LINE
LINE – COUNTER
LINES
LOCATION
LOCK
LOW – VALUE

LOW – VALUES
LOWER – BOUND
LOWER – BOUNDS

MEMORY
MINUS
MODE
MODULES
MOVE
MULTIPLE
MULTIPLIED
MULTIPLY

NEGATIVE
NEXT
NO
NOT
NOTE
NUMBER
NUMERIC

OBJECT – COMPUTER
OBJECT – PROGRAM
OCCURS
OF
OFF
OH
OMITTED
ON
OPEN
OPTIONAL
OR
OTHERWISE
OUTPUT
OV
OVERFLOW

PAGE
PAGE – COUNTER
PERFORM
PF
PH
PICTURE
PLACES
PLUS
POINT
POSITION
POSITIVE
PREPARED
PRIORITY
PROCEDURE
PROCEED
PROCESS

PROCESSING
PROGRAM – ID
PROTECT

QUOTE
QUOTES

RANDOM
RANGE
RD
READ
RECORD
RECORDING
RECORDS
REDEFINES
REEL
RELEASE
REMARKS
RENAMES
RENAMING
REPLACING
REPORT
REPORTING
REPORTS
RERUN
RESERVE
RESET
RETURN
REVERSED
REWIND
RF
RH
RIGHT
ROUNDED
RUN

SA
SAME
SD
SEARCH
SECTION
SECURITY
SEEK
SEGMENT – LIMIT
SELECT
SELECTED
SENTENCE
SEQUENCED
SEQUENTIAL
SET
SIGN
SIGNED

SIZE
SORT
SOURCE
SOURCE – COMPUTER
SPACE
SPACES
SPECIAL – NAMES
STANDARD
STATUS
STOP
SUBTRACT
SUM
SUPERVISOR
SUPPRESS
SYMBOLIC
SYNCHRONIZED

TALLY
TALLYING
TAPE
TERMINATE
THAN
THEN
THROUGH
THRU
TIMES
TO
TYPE

UNEQUAL
UNIT
UNTIL
UP
UPON
UPPER – BOUND
UPPER – BOUNDS
USAGE
USE
USING

VALUE
VALUES
VARYING

WHEN
WITH
WORDS
WORKING – STORAGE
WRITE

ZERO
ZEROES
ZEROS

Solutions and answers to exercises

Ch. 4

1. Data-names   a) b) f) i)
   Procedure-names a) b) e) f) i) j)

2. a) c) f) i)

3. a) MOVE ZERO TO ADD IF IS LESS THAN GO DISPLAY STOP RUN
   b) K TOTAL
   c) INIT NEW – K TERMINATION
   d) ZERO 1 100

Ch. 5

1. The result is given by the following table where new values are indicated by underlining:

	A	B	C	D	E
Before:	1	5	3	10	-7
a)	1	1	3	10	-7
b)	1	5	3	1	1
c)	15	5	3	10	-7
d)	1	5	9	10	-7
e)	1	5	8	10	-7
f)	1	5	3	11	-6
g)	19	5	3	10	-7
h)	1	3	3	10	-7
i)	1	5	3	5	-7
j)	1	5	3	5	5
k)	-5	5	3	10	-7
l)	1	5	15	10	-7
m)	3	15	9	10	-7
n)	1	5	3	10	30
o)	1	5	3	10	2
p)	1	-1	3	-2	-7
q)	1	5	3	10	2.5
r)	1	5	8	10	-7
s)	-16	5	3	-16	-7

2. a) ADD T S.
COMPUTE S = S + T.

b) MULTIPLY T BY T GIVING H. ADD H TO S.
COMPUTE S = S + T ** 2.

c) MULTIPLY P BY K GIVING H. ADD H A GIVING B.
COMPUTE B = P * K + A.

d) DIVIDE QUANT INTO COST GIVING H.
ADD PURCHASE-PRIZE H GIVING ITEM-PRIZE.

COMPUTE ITEM-PRIZE = PURCHASE-PRIZE + COST /
QUANT.

3. IF X LESS ZERO MOVE -1 TO SIGNUM
ELSE IF X EQUAL TO ZERO MOVE ZERO TO SIGNUM
ELSE MOVE 1 TO SIGNUM.

4. IF CODEX IS NOT ALPHABETIC GO TO ERROR-IN-DATA.

5. SUMMATION. COMPUTE SUM-1 = SUM-1 + 1 / K;
MOVE K TO R.

TERM-COMPUTATION. MOVE ZERO TO SUM-1.
PERFORM SUMMATION VARYING K FROM 1 BY 1
UNTIL SUM-1 IS GREATER THAN 10.
DISPLAY R.

6. PROCEDURE DIVISION.
START. MOVE ZERO TO SUM-1 SUM-OF-SQUARES TOTAL.
OPEN INPUT EXPERIMENT-FILE.
NEW-RECORD. READ EXPERIMENT-FILE
AT END GO TO PRINT-OUT.
IF OBS-X GREATER ZERO AND OBS-X LESS 10
NEXT SENTENCE ELSE GO TO NEW-RECORD.
ADD 1 TO TOTAL. ADD OBS-X TO SUM-1.
MULTIPLY OBS-X BY OBS-X GIVING OBS-X-SQ.
ADD OBS-X-SQ TO SUM-OF-SQUARES.
GO TO NEW-RECORD.
PRINT-OUT. DISPLAY TOTAL SUM-1 SUM-OF-SQUARES.
CLOSE EXPERIMENT-FILE. STOP RUN.

Ch. 6

1. 01   SALARY-SPECIFICATION
      02   EMP-NO
      02   NAME
      02   ADDR
      02   TO-DATE
            03   PREL-TAX
            03   GROSS-PAY
      02   EMOLUMENTS
            03   SALARY
            03   FEE
            03   VARIOUS
      02   DEDUCTIONS
            03   TAXES
                  04   PREL
                  04   ARREARS
            03   VARIOUS
      02   NET-PAY

2.

$$A \begin{cases} B \\ C \begin{cases} D \begin{cases} E \\ F \end{cases} \\ G \end{cases} \\ H \{ I \end{cases} \qquad A \begin{cases} B \\ C \begin{cases} D \begin{cases} E \\ F \end{cases} \\ G \{ H \{ I \end{cases} \end{cases}$$

3. Let N stand for numeric, AB for alphabetic, AN for alphanumeric.
   a) 2, N or AN b) 3, AB or AN c) 3, N d) 3, AN e) 3, N
   f) 5, AN g) 3, N h) 5, AN i) 2, AN j) 5, AB or AN
   k) 5, AN l) 6, AN

4. 12345 in all cases.

5. a) 3 N   1 0 2
   b) 3 N   1 2 3
   c) 5 N   1 2 3 4 5 0 0 0 0
   d) 1 N   0 0 1̄
   e) 1 N   1 0 0 0
   f) 1 N   0 1
   g) 6 AB BUSTER
   h) 3 AN B 6)
   i) 7 AN + + + - - 0 1

   j) 2 AN P .
   k) 3 AN 2 . 7
   l) 5 AN + 1 . 7 6
   m) 1 N   5 0
   n) 5 N   0 0 1 2 3 0
   o) 3 N   0 0 0 0 1̄
   p) 3 N   0 0 1 0 0̄
   q) 5 AN 1 2 K 2 1
   r) 1 AB F

6. a) 0 3   JOB-TIME PICTURE 99V99 .
   b) 0 5   LOAN PICTURE S9 (5) PPP .
   c) 0 2   COUNTY PICTURE A (8) .
   d) 1 0   A PICTURE SPP9 (4) .

7. a) Z Z Z . Z Z
   b) Z Z 9 9 9
   c) Z Z Z 9 9 . 9 9
   d) ∗ ∗ V ∗ ∗

8. Blanks are indicated by b.

   a) b b 9 . 0 0 , b b b . 0 1 , b b b b b b , 1 7 8 . 2 1
   b) b b 0 0 0 , b 1 1 7 4 , b b 0 1 0
   c) b b b 0 0 . 9 5 , b b 1 0 2 . 3 1 , b b b 0 0 . 0 0 , b b 7 1 0 . 0 0
   d) 4 8 3 4 , 1 5 0 0 , ∗ ∗ 2 7 , ∗ ∗ ∗ ∗ , ∗ ∗ 0 5

9. a) 0 2 7 0
   b) b b b b
   c) 0 0 . 1 1 3 0
   d) 0 0 1 1
   e) ∗ ∗ ∗ ∗ . ∗ ∗
   f) ∗ 0 1 2 0 0

   g) ∗ 0 0 0 1 2
   h)   7 1 9
   i)   2 3 0 . 9 5 0 0
   j) ∗ ∗ ∗ 0 2 1 . 4 1 2 0
   k) . 3 1
   l) ∗ . 3 1

142

10. a) 0 1 2 . 2 7 +   g) - 1 9 . 7 4 0
    b) 0 2 1 DB   h)   - . 0 7 5 0
    c) 0 1 2 +   i) $ 1 9 . 3 3 +
    d) -   . 0 7 5 0   j) $. 9 6
    e) b b b b   k) $ - 8 . 6 0
    f) $ 1 0 6 1   l) b b b b b b b

11. a) $ * * * , * * * . * * CR
    b) 9 9 B 9 9 B 9 9 , B 9 9 9
    c) - - - - , - - - . 9 9
    d) Z Z Z , 9 9 9 . 9 9 +

12. a) B A I N E S b b b b CHERRY
    b) B A I N E S CHERRY b b b b
    c) B A I N E S b b b CHERRY b b

13. 0 1   SALARY - SPECIFICATION .
         0 2   EMP - NO PICTURE IS 9 9 9 9 .
         0 2   NAME PICTURE IS A (2 0) .
         0 2   ADDR PICTURE IS X (2 0) .
         0 2   TO - DATE .
              0 3   PREL - TAX PICTURE IS Z Z , Z Z 9 .
              0 3   GROSS - PAY PICTURE IS Z Z , Z Z Z . 9 9 .
         0 2   EMOLUMENTS .
              0 3   SALARY PICTURE IS Z , Z Z Z . 9 9 .
              0 3   FEE PICTURE IS Z , Z Z Z . 9 9 .
              0 3   VARIOUS PICTURE IS Z , Z Z Z . 9 9 CR .
         0 2   DEDUCTIONS .
              0 3   TAXES .
                   0 4   PREL PICTURE IS Z , Z Z 9 CR .
                   0 4   ARREARS PICTURE IS Z , Z Z 9 CR .
              0 3   VARIOUS PICTURE IS Z , Z Z Z . 9 9 CR .
         0 2   NET - PAY PICTURE IS $ * , * * * . 9 9 CR .

14. a) FD   SUPPLIES
          LABEL RECORD IS STANDARD VALUE OF ID IS
          " SUPPLIES " DATA RECORD IS ARTICLE .

    b) FD   EMPLOYEES
          BLOCK CONTAINS 2 0 RECORDS
          LABEL RECORDS OMITTED
          DATA RECORDS ARE HOUR - EMP , WEEK - EMP ,
          MONTH - EMP .

15. b) c) e) f)

16. 0 1   SALARY - TABLE .
         0 2   S - CLASS OCCURS 3 2 .
              0 3   AMOUNT OCCURS 3 PICTURE 9 9 9 9 .

          AMOUNT (1 1 , 3)

143

```
1. ENVIRONMENT DIVISION.
   CONFIGURATION SECTION.
   SOURCE-COMPUTER. AJAX.
   OBJECT-COMPUTER. AJAX.
   INPUT-OUTPUT SECTION.
   FILE-CONTROL. SELECT F-FILE ASSIGN TO
       TAPE-UNIT-4 MULTIPLE REEL. SELECT OPTIONAL
       TRANSACTIONS ASSIGN TO CARD-READER.
       SELECT G-FILE ASSIGN TO PRINTER.
   I-O-CONTROL. RERUN ON DRUM EVERY REEL F-FILE.
```

Ch. 8

```
1. IDENTIFICATION DIVISION.
   PROGRAM-ID. SALARY-ROUTINE.
   AUTHOR. ANNA LYSEGARD.

   ENVIRONMENT DIVISION.
   CONFIGURATION SECTION.
   SOURCE-COMPUTER. AJAX.
   OBJECT-COMPUTER. AJAX.
   SPECIAL-NAMES. TOP-OF-FORM IS NEW-NOTICE.
   INPUT-OUTPUT SECTION.
   FILE-CONTROL.
       SELECT INPUT-MASTER ASSIGN TO TAPE-UNIT-1.
       SELECT OUTPUT-MASTER ASSIGN TO TAPE-UNIT-2.
       SELECT TRANS ASSIGN TO CARD-READER.
       SELECT NOTICE ASSIGN TO PRINTER.

   DATA DIVISION.
   FILE SECTION.
   FD  INPUT-MASTER LABEL RECORDS OMITTED
       DATA RECORD IS EMP-IN.
   01  EMP-IN.
       02 NR PICTURE 9999.
       02 NAME PICTURE X(40).
       02 ADDR PICTURE X(40).
       02 SALARY PICTURE 9999.
       02 ACC-SAL PICTURE 9(5).
   FD  OUTPUT-MASTER LABEL RECORDS OMITTED
       DATA RECORD IS EMP-OUT.
   01  EMP-OUT.
       02 NR-OUT PICTURE 9999.
       02 NAME-OUT PICTURE X(40).
       02 ADDR-OUT PICTURE X(40).
       02 SALARY-OUT PICTURE 9999.
       02 ACC-SAL-OUT PICTURE 9(5).
   FD  TRANS LABEL RECORDS OMITTED
       DATA RECORD IS TR.
   01  TR.
       02 NR-TR PICTURE 9999.
       02 CODE-NR PICTURE 99.
       02 CHANGE PICTURE 9999.
   FD  NOTICE LABEL RECORDS OMITTED
       DATA RECORDS ARE NAME-N, ADDR-N, SPEC.
   01  NAME-N PICTURE X(40).
   01  ADDR-N PICTURE X(40).
   01  SPEC.
       02 SALARY-N PICTURE ZZZ9.
       02 DIFF PICTURE +(6)9.
       02 ACT-SAL-N PICTURE $(6)9.
       02 ACC-SAL-N PICTURE Z(6)9.
```

144

```
WORKING-STORAGE SECTION.
77  ACT-SAL PICTURE 9999.
CONSTANT SECTION.
77  MAX-NR PICTURE 9999 VALUE IS 9999.

PROCEDURE DIVISION.
P1.  OPEN INPUT INPUT-MASTER, TRANS
     OUTPUT OUTPUT-MASTER, NOTICE.
P2.  READ TRANS AT END MOVE MAX-NR TO NR-TR.
P3.  READ INPUT-MASTER AT END GO TO P5.
     IF NR LESS NR-TR MOVE SALARY TO ACT-SAL
     GO TO P4. IF CODE-NR GREATER 49
     ADD CHANGE SALARY GIVING ACT-SAL
     ELSE SUBTRACT CHANGE FROM SALARY
     GIVING ACT-SAL.
     PERFORM P2.
P4.  ADD ACT-SAL ACC-SAL.
     WRITE EMP-OUT FROM EMP-IN.
     WRITE NAME-N FROM NAME
     AFTER ADVANCING NEW-NOTICE.
     WRITE ADDR-N FROM ADDR
     AFTER ADVANCING 2 LINES.
     MOVE SALARY TO SALARY-N.
     COMPUTE DIFF = ACT-SAL - SALARY.
     MOVE ACT-SAL TO ACT-SAL-N.
     MOVE ACC-SAL TO ACC-SAL-N.
     WRITE SPEC AFTER ADVANCING 4 LINES.
     GO TO P3.
P5.  CLOSE INPUT-MASTER, TRANS, OUTPUT-MASTER,
     NOTICE. STOP RUN.
```

The solution to exercise 2 is given on the next two pages.

```
2. IDENTIFICATION DIVISION.
   PROGRAM-ID. ELECTRICITY-ACCOUNTS.

   ENVIRONMENT DIVISION.
   CONFIGURATION SECTION.
   SOURCE-COMPUTER. ZEUS.
   OBJECT-COMPUTER. ZEUS.
   SPECIAL-NAMES. TOP-OF-FORM IS NEW-FORM.
   INPUT-OUTPUT SECTION.
   FILE-CONTROL.
       SELECT SUBSCRIBER-IN ASSIGN TO TAPE-1.
       SELECT SUBSCRIBER-OUT ASSIGN TO TAPE-2.
       SELECT ACCOUNTS ASSIGN TO PRINTER.
       SELECT CONSUMPTION ASSIGN TO CARD-READER.

   DATA DIVISION.
   FILE SECTION.
   FD   SUBSCRIBER-IN BLOCK CONTAINS 100 RECORDS
        LABEL RECORDS STANDARD
        DATA RECORD IS SUBSCR.
   01   SUBSCR.
        02   SUBS-NR PICTURE 9(6).
        02   NAME PICTURE X(40).
        02   ADDR PICTURE X(40).
        02   S-CLASS PICTURE 99 COMPUTATIONAL.
        02   METER-POS PICTURE 9(6).
        02   YTD-CONS PICTURE 9(5) COMPUTATIONAL.
   FD   SUBSCRIBER-OUT BLOCK CONTAINS 100 RECORDS
        LABEL RECORDS STANDARD
        DATA RECORD IS SUBSCR-OUT.
   01   SUBSCR-OUT.
        02   SUBS-NR-OUT PICTURE 9(6).
        02   NAME-OUT PICTURE X(40).
        02   ADDR-OUT PICTURE X(40).
        02   S-CLASS-OUT PICTURE 99 COMPUTATIONAL.
        02   METER-POS-OUT PICTURE 9(6).
        02   YTD-CONS-OUT PICTURE 9(5) COMPUTATIONAL.
   FD   CONSUMPTION LABEL RECORDS OMITTED
        DATA RECORD IS CONS.
   01   CONS.
        02 SUBS-NR-C PICTURE 9(6).
        02 METER-POS-C PICTURE 9(6).
   FD   ACCOUNTS LABEL RECORDS OMITTED
        DATA RECORDS ARE SUBSCRIBER, SPEC.
   01   SUBSCRIBER.
        02   SUBS-NR-A PICTURE 9(6).
        02   NAME-A PICTURE BBBX(40).
        02   ADDR-A PICTURE BBBX(40)BBB.
        02   S-CLASS-A PICTURE 99.
   01   SPEC.
        02   METER-POS-A.
             03   PREV-POS PICTURE 9(6).
             03   PRES-POS PICTURE 9(6).
        02   SUB-FEE PICTURE $$$9.99.
        02   CONS-CHARGE PICTURE $(5)9.99.
        02   AMOUNT PICTURE $(5)9.99.
   WORKING-STORAGE SECTION.
   77   DIFF PICTURE S9(6) COMPUTATIONAL.
   77   IND PICTURE 99 COMPUTATIONAL.
   77   TEMP PICTURE 9(5)V99 COMPUTATIONAL.
   77   RATE PICTURE V99 COMPUTATIONAL.
   01   TARIFF.
        02   FIXED-FEE PICTURE 999 COMPUTATIONAL
             OCCURS 10 TIMES.
```

146

```
CONSTANT SECTION.
77  MAX-POS PICTURE 9(7) COMPUTATIONAL
    VALUE IS 1000000.
77  MAX-NR PICTURE 9(6) VALUE IS 999999.


PROCEDURE DIVISION.
BEGIN. ACCEPT RATE.
    MOVE 1 TO IND PERFORM ACCEPT-TARIFF
    10 TIMES.
    OPEN INPUT SUBSCRIBER-IN CONSUMPTION
    OUTPUT SUBSCRIBER-OUT ACCOUNTS.
READ-CONS. READ CONSUMPTION AT END
    MOVE MAX-NR TO SUBS-NR-C.
READ-SUB. READ SUBSCRIBER-IN AT END
    GO TO TERMINUS.
    IF SUBS-NR LESS SUBS-NR-C
    WRITE SUBSCR-OUT FROM SUBSCR
    GO TO READ-SUB.
    MOVE SUBS-NR TO SUBS-NR-A
    MOVE NAME TO NAME-A
    MOVE ADDR TO ADDR-A
    MOVE S-CLASS TO S-CLASS-A
    WRITE SUBSCRIBER AFTER ADVANCING NEW-FORM.
    SUBTRACT METER-POS FROM METER-POS-C
    GIVING DIFF.
    IF DIFF LESS ZERO ADD MAX-POS TO DIFF.
    MULTIPLY DIFF BY RATE GIVING TEMP,
    CONS-CHARGE.
    ADD TEMP, FIXED-FEE (S-CLASS) GIVING AMOUNT.
    MOVE METER-POS TO PREV-POS
    MOVE METER-POS-C TO PRES-POS
    MOVE FIXED-FEE (S-CLASS) TO SUB-FEE
    WRITE SPEC AFTER ADVANCING 4 LINES.
    MOVE METER-POS-C TO METER-POS
    ADD DIFF TO YTD-CONS
    WRITE SUBSCR-OUT FROM SUBSCR.
    GO TO READ-CONS.
TERMINUS. CLOSE SUBSCRIBER-IN CONSUMPTION
    SUBSCRIBER-OUT ACCOUNTS.
    DISPLAY "ELECTRICITY-ACCOUNTS COMPLETED".
    STOP RUN.
ACCEPT-TARIFF.
    ACCEPT FIXED-FEE (IND) ADD 1 TO IND.
```

Index